fearless
knitting
WORKBOOK

fearless knitting
WORKBOOK

THE STEP-BY-STEP GUIDE TO KNITTING CONFIDENCE

jennifer e. seiffert

INTERWEAVE.
interweavestore.com

Editor Ann Budd
Technical Editor Lori Gayle
Photography Joe Coca
Illustrator Gayle Ford
Design nice kern, llc
Production Katherine Jackson

Interweave Press LLC
201 East Fourth Street
Loveland, CO 80537-5655 USA
interweavestore.com

Printed in China by Asia Pacific Offset, Ltd.

Library of Congress Cataloging-in-Publication Data

Seiffert, Jennifer E.
  Fearless knitting workbook : the step-by-step guide to
knitting confidence / Jennifer E. Seiffert, author.
      p. cm.
  Includes bibliographical references and index.
  ISBN 978-1-59668-149-1 (hardcover with concealed wire-o)
1. Knitting. I. Title.
  TT820.S445 2009
  746.43'2--dc22
                              2009011057

10 9 8 7 6 5 4 3 2 1

ACKNOWLEDGMENTS

Many knitting friends helped with this book, especially Kathy Carvey, owner of The Shuttle Shop in Warsaw, Indiana, my Local Yarn Shop. Kathy and Linda Arnold, Joan Barrette, Joanne Moore, and Kelly Warrick tested patterns, knit samples, and found mistakes and ambiguities. Their support was generous, and I am truly grateful.

Thanks also to Cascade Yarns Inc., for supplying yarn for many of the projects.

CONTENTS

All things are difficult
until they are easy.

INTRODUCTION

I often knit in airports and on planes, in doctors' offices, at the dentist while waiting for the anesthesia to take effect: whenever I am sitting and waiting. The most common question I'm asked when knitting in public is, "Is it hard?" I usually stumble or stutter some nonsense while really thinking that there is no answer to that question. Actually, one answer to this question was found in a fortune cookie: All things are difficult until they are easy. This book is my second answer to that question.

I have knitted for about forty-five years and have taught the advanced sweater class for my local yarn shop for several. I love knitting. I love the artistry of it and the ingenuity of complex possibilities created from simple elements. I love the sense of mastery and the "aha!" moment when the arcane symbols in the chart or instructions turn into amazing fabric. I love the physical rhythm of it, and I love the sensuous feel of yarn running through my fingers. I hope that my passion is contagious and that my students will find the same enthusiasm.

In class, I try to help my students understand the underlying construction principles so they have a foundation for the next challenge. I explain how everything in knitting is built from the same basic elements, and that nothing is beyond their capabilities. I've taken the same attitude in this book.

WHAT'S **DIFFERENT** ABOUT THIS BOOK?

This book is focused on helping you overcome a fear of knitting and gain self-confidence through a thorough understanding of the processes. Your understanding will deepen as you read the text and work through the exercises. The text will help your mind understand the principles behind the techniques and methods, while the exercises will help your hands get comfortable with the unfamiliar. Knitting is not as hard as you may think. I hope that after using this book you'll have the confidence to say, "I can make that!" in regard to any project you come across.

This book is a workbook in the sense that it consists of structured exercises that provide practice along with the concepts and techniques in different areas of knitting. In each skill area (knit-and-purl, shaping, cables, lace, and knitting in the round), skills are built step by step in a series of the exercises. The knitting instructions for each project use standard "knit-ese" abbreviations and symbols, but each is deconstructed and explained in detail. Many of the instructions are accompanied by a "why" statement, explaining the reason for the step; a chance to "read the knitting"; and tips that explain easier ways to execute the instructions.

The instructions and projects in this book assume you know the basics of how to cast on, knit, purl, and bind off, and how to knit garter stitch and stockinette stitch. It is also helpful to know how to read the information on yarn labels—suggested needle size and gauge, yarn weight, fiber content, and care instructions. This information can be found in the back of knitting books and magazines, or on the Internet.

It's important to note that the instructions and illustrations in this book are based on the English style of knitting, where the yarn is held in the right hand and thrown or wrapped around the left-hand needle. If you knit in the Continental method of holding the yarn in your left hand, you may need to make adjustments.

Your best knitting friends will be, well, your knitting friends—knitters you meet in classes or at your local yarn shop. Other friends you should cultivate include a comprehensive knitting reference book (or several) and the Internet. These will provide explanations of how to ssk, purl through the back loop, or perform most any technique when you're knitting at 2 a.m. The Internet can also provide endless inspiration and shopping opportunities and introduce you to other knitters through their blogs.

The techniques included in this book are the ones that you will encounter most frequently. A solid foundation of these techniques will give you the confidence to tackle projects in other books and magazines. For practicality, this book is limited to working with a single strand of working yarn (usually one color) at a time—there isn't space to include multicolor techniques.

This is not the only knitting book you'll ever need. There is a lifetime of things to learn beyond what's in these few pages. But don't let this intimidate you! It means that you need never be bored in your knitting life—knitting can take you in a million directions for as far as you want to go.

HOW TO USE THIS BOOK

You will get the most out of this book if you work through the exercises in the order that they appear. When new vocabulary or techniques are first introduced, they are explained and illustrated in some detail. This level of detail is not repeated when the words or techniques are used in later exercises. If you decide to work the projects out of order, I suggest you first at least read through the earlier sections. In each section, the exercises progress from the most basic presentation of the techniques to the most complex, ending with a challenging "extra credit" exercise.

Most of the exercises are based on knitting an 8" (20.5 cm) square. You can knit these squares as exercises only or transform them into useful projects. Four squares joined together can make a 16" (40.5 cm) pillow top front; eight can make a pillow front and back. Twenty squares (five rows of four squares) or more can make a baby blanket or throw. Individual squares knitted in cotton can be used as dishcloths or facecloths. Some of the squares can be continued in length to create a scarf.

Do you need to finish each square? That's up to you. If you work the squares simply to learn a new technique, you may choose to work only enough rows to reassure yourself that you can take on a larger project. However, if you work the squares to completion, you will gain practice and learn more about your own knitting style. The more you knit, the more you will experience a continual improvement in the regularity and smoothness of your stitches. You may discover that your gauge changes as you get comfortable with a technique.

Definitions

For the purpose of this book, I'll use the following definitions.

PROJECT
The knitted piece.

PATTERN
The stitch combinations or published instructions for a knitted piece.

RIGHT SIDE
The public side of the finished project.

WRONG SIDE
The non-public side of the finished project.

RIGHT-HAND SIDE
The side or edge of your knitting closest to your right hand.

LEFT-HAND SIDE
The side or edge of your knitting closest to your left hand.

NOTE
"Clockwise" and "counterclockwise" references will not be used because they are confusing (Which direction is the theoretical clock facing? Does it matter if I'm right-handed or left-handed? What time is it, anyway?).

For each project, the directions are divided into understandable sections.

INSTRUCTIONS The basic row-by-row instructions are first provided in standard knitting terminology, with all of the abbreviations, jargon, and funny symbols that can be so confusing to the beginner.

TRANSLATION If unfamiliar abbreviations or symbols are used in the instructions, a translation is given in understandable English.

WHY? This section explains the reason why something is to be done as instructed. Why does the pattern call for this many stitches? Why should you move the yarn this way and not that way?

TIP Wherever possible, I'll offer pointers to make the knitting easier.

READ YOUR KNITTING This section encourages you to see and understand the results of the instructions just performed. Learning to read your knitting as well as the pattern makes you truly fearless in your knitting!

SELECTING YARN

If your primary purpose is to knit the project squares as learning exercises, choose any smooth yarn of the weight specified in a solid light color. Avoid fuzzy, variegated (at least for the first try), thick-and-thin and bouclé (loopy) yarns, all of which will obscure the stitches.

I recommend using a three-ply wool yarn for the project squares (I used Cascade 220 for most of the samples in this book). Wool is elastic and forgiving of differences in your tension and can be successfully blocked. However, if you want to learn about different knitting fibers, work the squares in different yarns to see how they affect the finished look. For example, work one square with a three-ply wool and another with a single-ply or two-ply yarn to see the difference. The staff at your local yarn store can help you make selections.

If you intend to use the project squares as dishcloths or facecloths, use cotton, linen, or hemp instead. But be aware that that these plant fibers are inelastic and more difficult for a beginner to work with. You might want to knit a square in wool first to learn the technique, then knit it again with a less forgiving yarn. Be easy on yourself and don't introduce unnecessary complications into your learning. On the other hand, the small size of the project squares is ideal for trying out different yarns to see if you like them enough to use in a larger project, such as a sweater.

If you intend to combine several project squares into a blanket or throw that might need laundering, consider using a machine-washable yarn. If you intend to extend a project square into a scarf, which doesn't need frequent laundering, feel free to choose a yarn that is labeled "handwash" or "dry clean only."

TEN THINGS THAT MAKE KNITTING SEEM HARD

1 The technique is one you haven't learned yet Any project will be hard if you don't know the required techniques or if the instructions look like Greek to you. But it will only be hard until you learn what you need to know. To quote my favorite fortune cookie, "All things are difficult until they are easy."

2 It requires an exact gauge Although it takes time, there's no getting around knitting a gauge swatch (or several) if you want your project to turn out with the same dimensions as specified in the instructions. If you find that your gauge varies a lot when you knit, stick to projects where size (and gauge) isn't critical.

3 You don't have the optimum tools The needles and accessories you use, even the lamp by your knitting chair, can affect your knitting ease. Depending on the type of needles and yarn you use, the stitches may stick on the needles or slide off too easily. Use the tools that make knitting easiest for you.

4 It requires 100% attention all of the time Some patterns involve a lot of repetition and regularity that is easy to follow; others involve different stitch patterns or complex shaping that requires close attention. Decide if the amount of repetition and regularity match the amount of attention you want to give.

5 It involves more manual dexterity than you think you have Granted, some knitting techniques are awkward, and some yarns are more difficult to maneuver, but just like playing an instrument, it takes repetition and practice for your nerves and muscles to learn the new skill.

6 The pattern instructions make assumptions about your knowledge Patterns written for beginning and intermediate knitters usually include more detailed instructions than those designed for experienced knitters. Read through the instructions to make sure you understand all of the steps and ask for help if you don't.

7 The pattern has errors! Unfortunately, some patterns do have errors. Therefore, it's a good idea to check the designer's or publisher's website for errata and corrections to errors that have already been discovered.

8 It takes too long Large projects (afghans, shawls, etc.) or projects knitted with very thin yarn will take a long time. If you have limited time, choose small projects or ones that use thicker yarn and have fewer stitches.

9 You want to modify a project Modifications to patterns (altering a neckline, adding a different stitch pattern, etc.) may require more advanced math and garment-designing skills than you have. If you're not up to the task, select a project you can follow as written.

10 You just don't enjoy it There's no rule that says you have to enjoy every aspect of knitting. If you find yourself struggling, bored, anxious, or disappointed, take a break.

01

GENERAL ADVICE

Regardless of the knitting techniques you use or your level of experience, there are fundamental skills and insights that can reduce your frustration. The advice in this section applies to all projects you knit, from the first step of choosing the best materials to the last step of finishing the completed piece. As you build your repertoire of techniques, you'll want to acquire confidence-building skills along the way, such as "reading" your knitting and fixing mistakes. This chapter offers ideas about how to make your knitting easier and more successful.

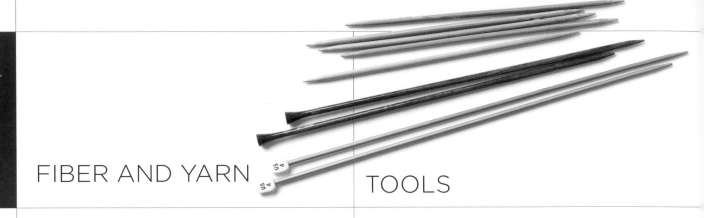

FIBER AND YARN

TOOLS

Some yarns and fibers are more difficult to work with than others. What makes them difficult? Many of the novelty yarns that were once so popular and that enticed new knitters are actually more difficult to work with than plain old wool. Multi-strand and railroad ribbon yarns tend to catch on your needles. Fuzzy yarns hide your stitches and make it hard to "read" your knitting or undo mistakes. Some yarns are fragile, making it hard to rip out and reknit.

The fiber that makes up a yarn plays a big part in knitting ease. Fibers differ in their elasticity, smoothness, how they have been processed into yarn, and many other factors. To learn more about fibers, how they are turned into yarn, and how to choose them for your projects, a wonderful place to start is *The Knitter's Book of Yarn: The Ultimate Guide to Choosing, Using, and Enjoying Yarn* by Clara Parkes (see Bibiography).

How is the insecure knitter to choose? In general, a good-quality smooth three-ply wool yarn in a light color is easiest to knit with. Yarns that are fuzzy, dark, inelastic (such as cotton, linen, and silk), change from thick to thin, or are loosely spun, are more difficult to manage. On the other hand, you may fall in love with a yarn that doesn't fall into the "easy" category. Your love for the yarn will keep you motivated, but if you find that knitting becomes too difficult, set the project aside. Gain some experience with an easier yarn to increase your confidence before you continue with the hard stuff. As with most things knitting, it's a good idea to discuss your yarn choice with your local yarn shop owner.

NEEDLES

There are so many choices of knitting needles today. All types of needles can be made from different materials: wood, metal, bamboo, plastic, or even glass, and points can have subtly different shapes.

STRAIGHT SINGLE-POINTED NEEDLES are made of a rigid material and have one pointed end and a stopper on the other end to keep the stitches from falling off. They are used to knit back and forth in rows. They come in different lengths, usually from 9" (23 cm) to 14" (35.5 cm). You can always use a needle longer than required, but you can't use one that is too short to hold all of the stitches in your project.

DOUBLE-POINTED NEEDLES are made from a rigid material, have (surprise!) two pointed ends, and come in sets of 4 or 5, from 4" (10 cm) to 10" (25.5 cm) long. They are used to knit in the round, or circularly, and are usually used for smaller projects like hats, socks, or baby items. One of the needles performs the work of the right-hand needle, and the others hold the stitches in what is actually more of a square or triangle than a circle. The needles take turns as the working needle. You can always use longer double-pointed needles than necessary, but you can't use needles that are too short to hold the stitches comfortably without stitches falling off.

CIRCULAR NEEDLES aren't actually circular, but they are used for circular knitting. They have two rigid pointed ends connected with a thin flexible cable and range from about 9" (23 cm) to 60" (152.5 cm) long. Circular needles can be used for back-and-forth or circular knitting. When knitting back and forth, you can use a circular needle longer than required. But when knitting in the round, the needle must be the right size for the project. Otherwise the stitches will either be too crowded or too stretched out. Sometimes the rigid parts are straight, and sometimes they are angled. One style may be

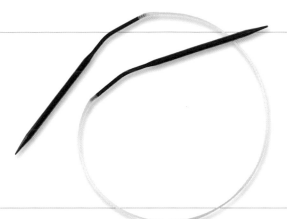

more comfortable for you than the other. (I like the angled ones because the bend fits right at my little finger.) When buying circular needles, always check the quality of the cable and the join where the cable and points are attached. Poor-quality cables can be too springy, and they will curl up awkwardly, fighting back instead of lying quietly. If the joins are poor, they will catch your stitches, which can be annoying.

FLEX NEEDLES are a hybrid, with a single rigid point attached to a cable with a stopper at the other end. They are used just like straight needles. Some of these come as sets of interchangeable lengths of cables and sizes of needle points, so you can customize the needles for each project.

So, what are the optimum needles for your project? Needle choice is very personal and your preferences may well vary with the yarn you're using, your skill level, and the project you're working on. Here are some examples of how you might select a specific needle for a specific project:

AN AFGHAN KNITTED IN ONE PIECE will be so wide that you will need a long circular needle to hold all of the stitches.

LACEWORK ON FINE YARN. Long, sharpish points will facilitate the stitch manipulations. Using a needle with a shortish blunt point will be very frustrating as you try, for example, to k3tog (knit three together). But if the points are very sharp and you tend to push them with your fingertips as you knit, you can draw blood!

SLICK SLIPPERY YARN. If the stitches tend to inadvertently slip off the needles, try using needles that have more "grab," such as wood, bamboo, or plastic, instead of metal.

LARGE SIZE NEEDLES. Size 17 (12 mm) needles made of wood are uncomfortably heavy, as I found out when I used them to knit a chunky novelty scarf. I felt as though I was doing weight training. Hollow metal or plastic needles will be lighter and easier to use in large sizes.

IF YOU HAVE ARTHRITIS, fibromyalgia, or another painful condition, try flexible plastic needles. They may be warmer than metal and cause less muscle tension.

BOTTOM LINE: If a project seems hard because the individual stitches are hard to work, or you find yourself having to pay too much attention to how the stitches sit on the needles, try a different type of needle.

Most of the projects in this book are knitted back and forth in rows. For these you can use straight, circular, or flex needles, as you prefer. Projects in the Going in Circles chapter are knitted in the round and require circular or double-pointed needles.

I recommend that you buy the best quality needles you can afford, especially in the most basic sizes and lengths. Your needles can last your lifetime and beyond. I still use knitting needles and crochet hooks that belonged to my grandmother. Good tools will enhance the pleasure of the craft. The more experienced you become, the more sensitive you will be to differences in needles. You will be glad you bought the best in the first place.

ACCESSORIES

Some accessories are essential, others are nice to have, and some you may try once and never use again. Many essential accessories are actually office supplies. I assume you already have pens, pencils, highlighters, and scissors, so here's a shopping list for the other essentials.

STITCH MARKERS in different sizes (to fit different size needles), both closed rings and locking markers. Their uses will be covered in the projects later in the workbook.

RIGID RULERS OF VARYING LENGTHS. Measuring on a hard surface with a rigid ruler is more accurate than measuring on your knee or the arm of a chair with a tape measure. Keep a 6" (15 cm) ruler (my favorite are the metal sewing/knitting gauges with movable pointers shown in the discussion of gauge swatches on page 21) with your in-process project. Have a 12" (30.5 cm) ruler and a yard stick handy, too.

CROCHET HOOKS for fixing mistakes, weaving in ends, and substitute cable needles. The size often doesn't matter. It's the hook that is so useful.

STICKY NOTES to use to keep your place in a chart.

YARN OR TAPESTRY NEEDLES for weaving in ends and sewing seams. Make sure the eye is large enough to thread with yarn. True tapestry needles have blunt points, which are ideal for knitting because they don't pierce the yarn, but sharp-point needles can also work. Some needles have bent tips, others are straight. Either type will work, and you will develop preferences over time.

PHOTOCOPY OF YOUR PATTERN. Make a copy on which you can make notes and highlight the instructions for the size you are making. This saves you from carrying a magazine or book around when you take your knitting with you. A photocopy for personal use is acceptable under copyright rules.

In addition, the following are also useful. Quality needles are expensive and their loss is both costly and frustrating (such as when you can't sleep and want to cast on that cashmere hat at 2 a.m. but can't find the right needle). So buy a good needle case or use a basket, box, or other container and always put your needles back when you're done using them.

MAGNETIC EASELS are a great way to hold a pattern or chart upright and to keep your place as you work.

STITCH HOLDERS are rigid "safety pins" that act as parking lots for your stitches when you take them off the needles. Sometime they are necessary partway through a piece.

If you want to use your needles for something else before a project is finished, you can put your in-progress work on a stitch holder. I put stitch holders in the nonessential category because you can improvise by threading the stitches on a length of contrasting waste yarn.

CABLE NEEDLES (SHOWN AT TOP OF PAGE) discussed in the cable chapter. They are nice to have, but because you can substitute other tools, they are not essential.

STITCH OR ROW COUNTERS are used to keep track of stitches and rows worked. There are many types, but all require pushing a button or turning a dial to record completed steps or repeats or rows. Although many knitters like them, I forget to push the button and can never trust the count they show. I end up "reading my knitting" anyway. In this workbook, I'll give you tips for reading the counts from your knitting itself. But if a counter will help you, by all means use one. You can also improvise by making hatch marks on paper.

CALCULATORS are helpful if you need to do some math—for example, if you want to change the length of a sleeve or work a pattern at a different gauge.

NEEDLE GAUGES are handy for determining the size of unmarked needles. Simply insert your needle through the best-fit hole to find out its size. Most needle gauges give sizes in U.S. and metric systems.

KNITTING BAGS AND TOOL HOLDERS can range in cost from nothing to hundreds of dollars. Why not start with the freebies until you know what you like and need? For a bag to hold a project (yarn, work in progress, pattern, and accessories) try a clear plastic zipper-top bag, such as the type that bedding is sold in. For me, a zip-top is essential to keep out curious cats. For holding stitch markers, use a small tin that breath mints or chocolates are sold in (go ahead and buy one just so you can eat the chocolates). My favorite accessory holder has room for two of these tins, plus a 6" (15 cm) ruler, tape measure, pencils, sticky notes, needle gauge, stitch holders, cable needles, and tapestry needles. It's a cosmetic bag that I was given when I purchased something a lot less useful than the container it came in. It even has elastic bands (originally intended to hold make-up brushes) that keep my hooks and holders neatly arranged.

REFERENCE BOOKS & INTERNET SITES

It's a good idea to have one or more general knitting reference books that cover techniques and basic information. The Bibliography on page 158 lists some books that I rely on.

The Internet is an astonishing resource—all things knitting all the time. The information available can be overwhelming in content and variety of media (text, photos, videos) and approach (commercial sites, blogs, social networking), so start by using a search engine like Google—just type in whatever you are interested in. But be forewarned, you may lose yourself in it for hours once you get started.

ENVIRONMENT

LEARN YOUR OWN KNITTING STYLE

Maybe this section will seem obvious, but when you're learning a new knitting skill, it is helpful to have a quiet place with good lighting and no interruptions for at least a half hour. For me, that has meant getting a color-corrected fluorescent floor lamp designed for crafting at my knitting chair. It means keeping the cats away from my lap for the time needed to read and understand a new pattern and get started. It also means putting a phone near my knitting chair so I don't have to get up mid row to answer a call. For some of you, it may mean getting magnifying reading glasses. It's helpful to have a table within easy reach with a stand or easel for your pattern or book so you can have it upright and be able to refer to it from your chair without taking your hands away from your needles. And if you are using long straight needles, avoid sitting in a chair with arms that get in the way of your needles, or try shorter needles, or circular needles.

Each knitter has her or his own style. We each knit for our own reasons; we achieve satisfaction from different aspects of the craft. Some of us are oriented to the finished product. Others of us enjoy the process of knitting as much as the final result. As you begin your knitting adventure, you are free to discover and follow your own style. Pay attention what inspires you and do more of that. Acknowledge what bores you and do less of that.

For me, knitting is a refuge from stress and a focus of my creativity. In my work, I spend a lot of time and energy thinking, analyzing, writing, and talking. Knitting is a rhythmic meditative activity into which I can relax my hands and mind to restore some balance. This means that I like to work on projects with a regular rhythm to the stitches. If the rows are too short, the flow is interrupted. If the pattern is too irregular, the flow is interrupted. So I have gravitated toward lace knitting, where I can work long rows of the same stitch sequence and create something beautiful. As much as I love cables, I avoid working them these days because they interrupt the flow. I can't stand modular knitting (too many small pieces knit onto each other, such as patch-work) because the rows are all short. I've come to recognize that this is all part of my knitting style and is unique to me. You will discover your own.

GAUGE SWATCHES

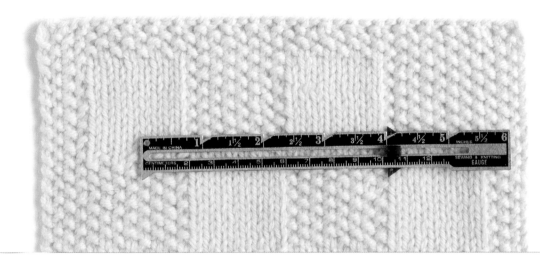

It's easy to count the number of stitches in blocks of stitch patterns.

The standard measurements for gauge are given in terms of 4" (10 cm). A gauge swatch should be a bit larger than that to give a full 4" (10 cm) of knitting to measure, away from the edge stitches. The pattern instructions you are working from should tell you what stitch pattern was used to establish the gauge. You must work your swatch in the specified pattern to get the same results. Usually the gauge is given for the pattern stitch used in the project, but sometimes the gauge is measured over stockinette stitch. The instructions may say to measure the gauge of your stitches "slightly stretched." They may provide instructions for washing or blocking your swatch. Be sure to follow any instructions provided before you measure your final gauge.

Always measure your gauge, or your knitting, on a flat rigid surface. Never measure it against your knee or the curved arm of an stuffed chair or sofa. Use a rigid ruler.

My favorite is a metal "Sewing and Knitting Gauge" with a movable pointer that can be set at the desired measurement. It makes it harder to fudge measurement on partial stitches. But believe it or not, I've found some of the cheaper versions of this type of ruler with the markings inaccurate. So check your bargain ruler against a trusted ruler or tape measure.

Measure the swatch while there is no stress on the stitches. It's important that the stitches are measured in a relaxed state, not compressed or stretched. If you are using a circular needle, slide the stitches to the flexible cable part of the needle and weigh down the rigid needle tips to prevent the cable from curling. Measure the stitches away from the edges and away from the needle.

It can be hard to count individual stitches. Sometimes you can use the number of stitches in a pattern repeat to help you count. In the photo above, the pattern stitch

It's more difficult to count the number of stitches in patterns that zigzag.

repeats over 8 stitches and a 4" (10 cm) width is represented by two 8-stitch blocks plus 4 additional stitches for a total of 20 stitches (5 stitches per inch). The stitch pattern in the photo above also repeats over 8 stitches, but it's less clear because the first stitch of one peak also serves as the last stitch of the previous peak. A complete peak is composed of 9 stitches instead of the 8 stitches in the repeat. Don't let this confuse your counting.

Because the project squares in this book are only 8" (20.5 cm) wide, a gauge swatch isn't really necessary. Instead, cast on the specified number of stitches and simply measure your gauge on the knitted square. Most knitting instructions will tell you to bind off the stitches and block the swatch before measuring the gauge. But for the small projects in this book that don't need to be specific dimensions, you can take the unorthodox approach of measuring the gauge while the piece is on the needles.

HOW DO YOU "GET GAUGE"?

The goal is to have the gauge of your swatch match that given in the pattern instructions you are working with so that you get predictable results. Start your swatch with the needle size suggested in the pattern. After you have knitted a couple of inches, take a preliminary stitch and row gauge measurement. If you are really far off, rip out and start again or simply switch to a different needle size and keep going. Be sure to mark the row where you change needle size so you won't mistakenly measure the wrong part again. If your measurements seem close, keep knitting with the same needles until you've worked at least 4" (10 cm) in length. Take gauge measurements again. If the pattern instructs you to treat the swatch before measuring, then bind off the stitches and block, wash, or do whatever the instructions say to do and re-measure to make sure you are on target.

If you are not going to block the swatch, don't bind off the stitches. Instead, put the swatch on a stitch holder or another set of needles of the same size. When I knit a sweater or shawl, I like to keep the gauge swatch on the needles so it's available for practicing any tricky bits like new stitch patterns. I can also use it to practice different-sized buttonholes or to check the size of needles to use to pick up stitches. If you don't have extra needles of the same size, put your gauge swatch on a stitch holder, then place it back on needles when you want to test a new stitch pattern, etc.

As you gain experience, you may discover that you always seem to knit tighter or looser than the pattern gauge, and you always need larger or smaller needles. If you anticipate this is true, begin your swatch with a larger or smaller needle in the first place.

HOW DO YOU KNOW WHAT SIZE NEEDLE TO SWITCH TO?

This can be confusing. If your gauge number is smaller than the pattern gauge, then you need to try a smaller needle. If your gauge number is larger, you need to try a larger needle. Let's think this through with an example. Let's say I'm working a swatch for a pattern that is written for 5 stitches to the inch and 7 rows to the inch. I start knitting a swatch with the suggested size 8 needles, and it measures 6 stitches per inch and 8 rows per inch. This means my stitches are too small (more of them fit in an inch that the pattern calls for). Therefore, I should try the next size needles—size 9—and swatch again. If my swatch measured 4½ stitches per inch instead of 5, my stitches would be too large (fewer fitting in an inch than the pattern calls for). In that case, I

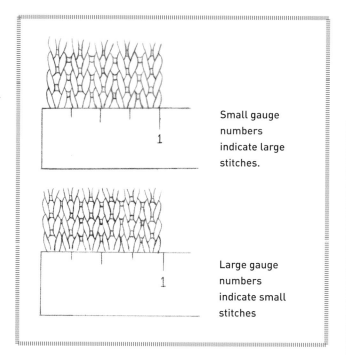

Small gauge numbers indicate large stitches.

Large gauge numbers indicate small stitches

should try a smaller needle—size 7—and swatch again. The size needle you end up using does not matter, as long as you are getting the gauge you need.

Gauge can be hard to match when you are substituting a different yarn from the one the designer used. Effective yarn substitution deserves several chapters in another book. If you have any questions about yarn, I suggest you consult the professionals at your local yarn shop. But don't consult them and then go elsewhere to purchase your yarn!

READ YOUR KNITTING

STITCH MOUNT

Reading your knitting means being able to look at your work and understand what you did based on what you see. This is invaluable in removing the fear factor from knitting because it removes that sense of knitting as mysterious, replacing it with self-confident assurance. This workbook is focused on helping you gain this skill. The best advice is to be conscious of this as a goal. Take time as you knit to relate any technique you work to its results. Think about how these results compare to the results from a related technique. Reading your knitting involves an analytic attitude of curiosity.

Stitch mount refers to how the stitches sit on the needles. Understanding stitch mount is one of the most important skills a knitter can learn because it is key to reading your knitting. Once you understand how the yarn is shaped into stitches and how the stitches are shaped into fabric, you can avoid mistakes, recognize them once they've been made, and fix them without fear!

I spent much of my knitting life not really understanding how knitting works. I could purl, and I could knit through the back loop, but I didn't understand why these two maneuvers weren't the same. Why is a purl stitch considered the reverse of a knit stitch, but knitting through the back loop isn't? Why is it called "the back loop" when there is only one loop involved? And I couldn't have explained to someone what knitting through the back loop accomplishes or why a purl looks the way it does. In short, I didn't really understand the difference between a knit and purl stitch. In the last few years, I discovered two books by creative experts that illuminated these issues: *Confessions of a Knitting Heretic* by Annie Modesitt and *Knitting in the Old Way* by Priscilla A. Gibson-Roberts and Deborah Robson. Both of these amazing books have much more to offer than discussions of stitch mounts, but they do discuss how stitches sit on the needles. I didn't experience that "aha" moment until I examined the knitted fabric once the stitches were off the needle.

It's important to note here that the following discussion is based on the knitting method used most commonly in Western Europe and North America. Other knitting traditions popular in different parts of the world involve stitches that are worked and mounted differently. Both of the books mentioned discuss some of these other traditions.

Let's start by looking at an illustration of stockinette-stitch fabric off of the needles. To form a row of knit stitches, the working yarn lies behind the completed work (away from the knit-stitch side), and the loops are pulled through to the front. To form a row of purl stitches, the work is turned around so the other side is facing you and the working yarn lies in front, and the loops are pulled through to the back. The two maneuvers are exactly the same! The working yarn is on one side of the fabric and the loops are pulled through to the other side.

Things get really interesting (read that, more geometrically complex) when the stitches are on needles. When the stitches are on needles, they are no longer parallel to the finished fabric. Instead, they lie at an angle almost, but not quite, perpendicular to the fabric. Think about how you would insert a needle into the stitches to get them all mounted on the needle facing in the same direction—you'll realize you have two choices. You could either stick the needle from front to back, pointing the needle away from you, or from back to front, pointing toward you. If you are working from right to left, inserting your needle from back to front of each stitch will get them lined up the same and in the correct stitch mount position for our Western knitting tradition. If you are working from left to right, you need to insert your needle into the front of each stitch to accomplish the same stitch mount.

When the stitches are mounted correctly, the yarn in the loops on the needles is closer to your right hand in the front of the needle and closer to your left hand at the back of the needle. If you hold the needle vertically and stretch the stitches apart, you can see the spiral path of the yarn more clearly. The spiral is in the direction of the letter Z rather than S (see page 28).

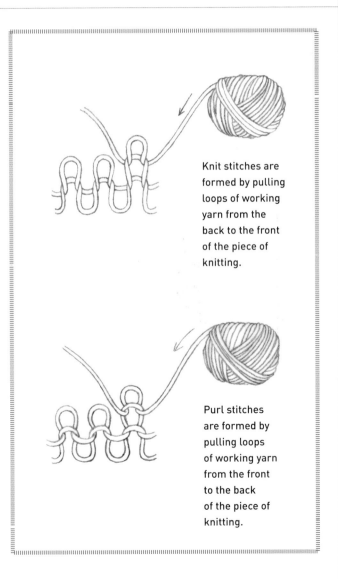

Knit stitches are formed by pulling loops of working yarn from the back to the front of the piece of knitting.

Purl stitches are formed by pulling loops of working yarn from the front to the back of the piece of knitting.

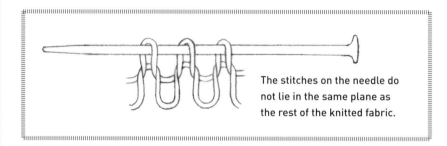

The stitches on the needle do not lie in the same plane as the rest of the knitted fabric.

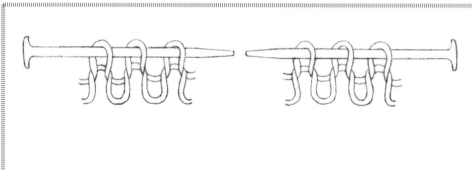

Working from left to right, the needle goes through the stitches from front to back; working from right to left, the needle goes through the stitches from back to front. The stitch mount is the same in both cases.

The difference between garter-stitch fabric and stockinette-stitch fabric has to do with how rows are sequenced—the stitch formation is the same. If succeeding rows are formed with the working yarn on the same side of the fabric, the fabric will be stockinette. If rows alternate which side the working yarn is on, the fabric will be garter stitch. When knitting back and forth, we turn the work at the end of each row and position the working yarn on the side closer to us (for purling) or farther away from us (for knitting). When working in the round, the work isn't turned, because there are no rows.

The same side of the fabric is always facing you. To create stockinette stitch in the round, you just keep knitting, keeping the yarn on the same side of the fabric (away from you). To create garter stitch, you will have to alternate knit and purl rounds, moving the yarn to the other side of the fabric between rounds.

When knit and purl stitches are to be worked on the same row, as in ribbing or other knit/purl patterns, you must keep repositioning the yarn either to the front or back as you work the row.

Now the difference between a purl and a knit through the back loop can be explained (at least I'll try!). But before I can explain that, I need to introduce another meaning of "front" and "back." In this section, I'll refer to the front and back surfaces of a stitch. Imagine the stitches off of the needle—the "front" is the surface of the stitches that faces you and is white; the "back" is the surface of the stitches that faces away from you and is shaded gray.

To form a purl stitch, the yarn is held in front of your needles and the right needle is inserted into the stitch in the back-to-front direction pointing toward you, and it is inserted from the back surface to the front surface of the stitch (from the shaded side toward the unshaded side). To "knit in the back loop," the yarn is held behind your needles (as usual for a knit stitch), and the needle is not inserted in a front-to-back direction as for a typical knit stitch, but it is inserted from the back (shaded) surface toward the front (unshaded) surface to twist the stitch—which means that the surface of the stitch that would normally face front (the unshaded surface in this example) has been turned to face the back and the surface facing forward is now the back (shaded) surface, as shown in the illustration on page 28. In case this isn't complicated enough, notice that it is the stitch in the row below the new one that actually gets twisted!

Purling through the back loop is somewhat harder to perform. Remember that our yarn will be in front for purling. The needle would ordinarily be inserted in a back-to-front direction, but now the needle must be inserted from the front (unshaded) surface of the stitch toward the back (shaded) surface. To do this, your right needle needs to go all the way over to the left-hand side of the stitch and come through the stitch from left to right in the back-to-front direction.

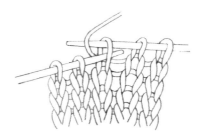

KNIT THROUGH THE BACK LOOP (K1TBL)
Holding the yarn in back, insert the right needle into the back loop of the first stitch on the left needle from front to back, then wrap the yarn around the needle to knit it as usual, thereby twisting the stitch.

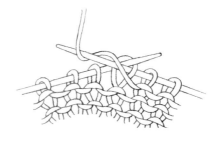

PURL THROUGH THE BACK LOOP (P1TBL)
Holding the yarn in front, insert the right needle into the back loop of the first stitch on the left needle from back to front, then wrap the yarn around the needle to purl it a usual, thereby twisting the stitch.

Why is this important? Making twisted stitches, or differently mounted stitches, is intentional in several situations.

"MAKE 1" (M1) AND "MAKE 1 PURLWISE" (M1P) INCREASES (SEE PAGES 78 AND 65, RESPECTIVELY). Working the new stitch through the back loop twists and tightens it so the increase doesn't leave a hole.

"KNIT IN FRONT AND BACK" (K1F&B) INCREASES (SEE PAGE 85). This is a way to make 2 stitches from 1, by first knitting into the front as usual and then knitting into the back loop, without dropping the stitch off the left needle until both new stitches have been formed.

SLIPPING STITCHES "AS IF TO KNIT" OR "KNITWISE." Sometimes, such as when forming certain decreases, a pattern will call for a stitch mount to be changed without working a stitch. The default way of slipping stitches (moving them from the left needle to the right needle without working them) is to insert the right needle from back to front, as though you were purling. Slipping "as if to knit" changes the stitch mount.

DECORATIVE STITCHES. Stitches knitted through the back loop against a purl background really stand out and are used in techniques such as Austrian or Bavarian traveling stitches.

Unintentional twisted or mis-mounted stitches happen, well, unintentionally, such as when you drop a stitch and pick it up mounted incorrectly. When you drop stitches, pick them up onto your needle however you can and then go back and check the stitch mount and rearrange stitches if needed before you work them. Or, as you become really confident, you can leave the stitches mis-mounted and when you come to them, work the mis-mounted stitches through the back loop to fix the mount—working a mis-mounted stitch through the back loop will untwist it!

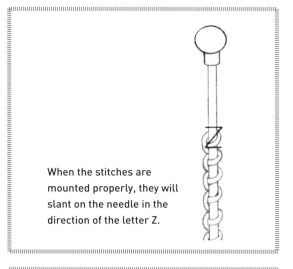

When the stitches are mounted properly, they will slant on the needle in the direction of the letter Z.

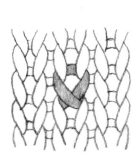

When a stitch is knitted through the back loop, the back surface (shaded gray) will face forward and the stitch will be twisted.

FINISHING SKILLS

WEAVING IN ENDS

When you have completed a project, you will need to weave in the ends of the yarn tails left from the cast-on and bind-off rows and anywhere else that you have joined in a new yarn. Although there are other ways to deal with weaving in ends (check a reference book or the Internet for details on splicing, knitting in tails as you go, etc.), I'll assume you're using a tapestry needle for the purposes of this book. It helps to keep two principles in mind when weaving in ends.

WEAVE IN THE ENDS SECURELY so they do not ravel during use or cleaning. Weave an end in one direction, then go back in the opposite direction for a few stitches to anchor the tail. Sometimes, I also like to split the yarn of the stitches being woven into, for added security.

WEAVE THE ENDS IN SO THAT THEY ARE INVISIBLE FROM THE RIGHT SIDE. For a piece that will be seamed, weave the tails in the seam allowance. If there is no seam allowance, weave the tail into the fabric, matching the direction the yarn was coming from or going toward to prevent a hole from forming. Put just enough tension on the yarn tail so that the join can't be seen on the right side—pulling too tightly will make the fabric pucker. Weave into solid areas, not openwork. Weave diagonally if that will make the result more invisible. If you are weaving in multiple tails near the same spot, weave them in different directions so the fabric doesn't become too thick in one place. I like to weave over and under a few stitches pulling the tail snug, then stretching the fabric to allow the tail to achieve the length it will need to maintain elasticity.

The swatch on page 30 shows the right and wrong side of a swatch worked in two colors to illustrate weaving in ends. The woven-in ends are hard to see on the right side of the knitting. Can you spot the ends on the wrong side? The cast-on end was woven vertically into the lower right edge on the wrong side, and the bind-off end was woven vertically into the upper left edge. The blue yarn was joined in at the middle of a row in the center of the piece, and its end was extended toward the direction it came from. The white end on the same row is woven the direction it would have continued in. The blue was switched back to white at the end of a row, so the blue end could be woven in vertically into the garter stitch on the upper right on the wrong side. The white end at the same spot needed to go in a different direction to prevent the fabric from becoming too thick. Weaving it vertically downward would have taken it into a stockinette section on an edge, which is difficult to conceal, so I wove that one horizontally.

The wrong side of the swatch also shows five short blue tails woven into the white fabric as examples of different directions and placements the yarn ends might take. If they were worked in the same color, all of these would be invisible from the right side of the piece.

Check the appearance from the right side before you cut the tail. If you need to readjust the yarn, unthread the needle and pull the yarn backward from the beginning of the tail, rethread the needle, and try again until you are satisfied with the result. Then cut the tail close to the fabric. However, if you are working with a lace piece, do not cut the tail until after blocking because all of the stretching the piece will undergo will change the position of the tail.

Right side of swatch with ends woven in.

Wrong side of swatch with ends woven in.

BLOCKING

Blocking is the process of applying moisture to a knitted fabric to relax the yarn, then shaping it as desired, and letting it dry. Blocking makes your knitting look its best—it evens out the stitches and allows the fibers to bloom, and it gives you a chance to learn how the yarn behaves. There are a number of ways to block knitting, depending on the fiber in the yarn and personal opinion. Check the yarn label for care instructions and check a reference book or your local yarn shop for advice if you use an unfamiliar yarn. For the purposes of the exercises in this workbook, I'll assume you are working with a yarn that can be handwashed (some can be machine washed—check the yarn label).

In a sink or basin, run a few inches of water of a temperature somewhere between cool and lukewarm or tepid. (I tried to find standard definition of these terms without success. I think the definitions may differ in cooking and bathing uses, as well. For reference, if a yarn label says to handwash in 30° water, that is 30° centigrade, or 86° Fahrenheit, cooler than body temperature; 40° centigrade is 104° Fahrenheit, warmer than body temperature.) I test the water temperature on my hands and wrists and use water slightly warmer than body temperature, but cooler than would be comfortable for bathing. I make note of the position of my single-handle faucet when the correct temperature is reached. Why do we care so much? Many yarns can felt (the fibers mat and bind together) if the water is too hot. I've never ever had problems with something felting unintentionally while being blocked, so don't stress too much over this, but do avoid hot water.

Add a small amount of liquid wool wash—maybe a teaspoon—then add the knitted piece. Gently smoosh the piece to get it fully wet but don't agitate it or rub it, which might also induce felting. Let it soak for at least 10 minutes, then check to see if any dye has colored the water (this will alert you to potential problems you may have with colorfastness). Let the water drain out of the sink and very gently squeeze (do not twist or wring) the piece to remove water. Remove the piece from the sink in a bundle (do not let it hang and stretch). Fill the sink with rinse water of the same temperature, then put the piece back in to rinse it. Again, squeeze out the water very gently, then roll the piece in a clean dry towel and let it set for a few minutes. Pin the piece to shape on a flat padded moisture-safe surface (such as an ironing board or carpeted floor) with rustproof pins inserted vertically through the piece into the padded surface. Let the piece dry completely before removing the pins.

I like to use a blocking board that is covered with a cloth printed with 1" (2.5 cm) checks. I use the checks to align the edges of my pieces and ensure that the corners are sharp. For blocking the 8" (20.5 cm) squares in this book, consider using a permanent marker to draw an 8" (20.5 cm) square on your blocking surface for a guide. Test the permanency of the marking with a scrap of fabric before placing your knitting on it!

SEAMS

When you knit a project that requires seams, spend some time investigating the best seam techniques in different situations, because the wrong choice of technique can detract from the finished appearance.

ASSESSING MISTAKES

When must you fix mistakes, and when can you leave them alone? This may be more of a question for Dr. Phil than for your knitting teacher. I've had students who had to fix absolutely every mistake or problem and would rather rip out and re-knit their work several times than leave a mistake in place. Then there are other students (fewer in number) who are very relaxed about mistakes. I myself am a recovering perfectionist, who eventually learned that "done is better than perfect."

The best knitting teachers will tell you, "There are no knitting police." This is true and in that spirit, here are my thoughts about when to fix mistakes.

WHEN THE MISTAKE AFFECTS THE STRUCTURE OR SIZE OF THE FINISHED PIECE. For example, if the right and left fronts of the sweater aren't the same length or if your gauge is off, and the garment is not going to fit.

WHEN THE MISTAKE CASCADES INTO MORE AND MORE PROBLEMS. A missed yarnover in a lace pattern affects the stitch count, which destroys the lace pattern in subsequent rows.

WHEN FIXING THE MISTAKE WILL BE AN OPPORTUNITY TO LEARN HOW TO DO IT RIGHT. Self explanatory.

WHEN THE PROJECT IS A GIFT AND THE MISTAKE WILL BE DISCOVERABLE BY THE RECIPIENT. Have enough respect for the recipient to do your best work. But if the recipient is a young boy who doesn't care if all the cables don't cross in the same direction, you needn't care either.

ABBREVIATIONS

beg(s)	begin(s); beginning
BO	bind off
cm	centimeter(s)
cn	cable needle
CO	cast on
cont	continue(s); continuing
dec(s)	decrease(s); decreasing
dpn	double-pointed needles
foll	follow(s); following
g	gram(s)
inc(s)	increase(s); increasing
k	knit
k1f&b	knit into the front and back of same stitch
kwise	knitwise, as if to knit
m	marker(s)
mm	millimeter(s)
M1	make one (increase)
p	purl
p1f&b	purl into front and back of same stitch
patt(s)	pattern(s)
psso	pass slipped stitch over
pwise	purlwise, as if to purl
rem	remain(s); remaining
rep	repeat(s); repeating
rev St st	reverse stockinette stitch
rnd(s)	round(s)

RS	right side
sl	slip
sl st	slip st (slip 1 stitch purlwise unless otherwise indicated)
ssk	slip 2 stitches knitwise, one at a time, from the left needle to right needle, insert left needle tip through both front loops and knit together from this position (1 stitch decrease)
st(s)	stitch(es)
St st	stockinette stitch
tbl	through back loop
tog	together
WS	wrong side
wyb	with yarn in back
wyf	with yarn in front
yd	yard(s)
yo	yarnover
*	repeat starting point
* *	repeat all instructions between asterisks
( )	alternate measurements and/or instructions
[ ]	work instructions as a group a specified number of times

DIAMOND PEAKS SQUARE, PAGE 48

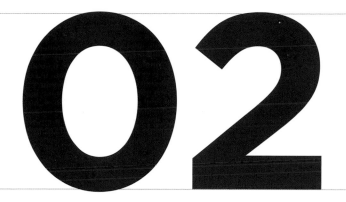

GETTING STARTED
KNIT AND PURL

Many interesting and beautiful patterns are formed with arrangements of just the knit and purl stitches you already know. They can be overall textures or isolated pictorial designs. Ribbing is a knit-and-purl pattern, with a regular repeat of knits and purls forming vertical ridges. Knit-and-purl patterns are the foundation of traditional "gansey" fisherman sweaters. This section will teach you to manage variations of knitting and purling and will bring a large variety of projects within your reach.

The instructions that follow use relatively standard abbreviations, which are provided on page 33. Written instructions will become much easier once you're familiar with these abbreviations.

Rib Sampler

FINISHED SIZE

About 7½" (19 cm) wide
and 3" (7.5 cm) long.

MATERIALS

+ Worsted-weight yarn
(#4 Medium).
SHOWN HERE Cascade 220 Wool
(100% wool; 220 yards
[201 meters]/100 grams):
#7829 red.

+ Size U.S. 5 (3.75 mm)
needles or size needed to
obtain gauge (I used size
U.S. 6 [4 mm] needles
because I tend to knit tightly).

WHY? Ribbing is often
worked with a needle two
sizes smaller than the
size otherwise used for the
yarn to keep the fabric
snug. Other projects in this
workbook will recommend
size U.S. 7 (4.5 mm) needles
for the same yarn.

+ 3 stitch markers.

+ Tapestry needle.

+ Pins for blocking.

GAUGE

28 stitches and 28 rows =
4" (10 cm); 7 stitches
and 7 rows = 1" (2.5 cm)
in ribbing, un-stretched.

TIP Ribbing gauge is often
specified for the fabric
"slightly stretched."
I'm never sure that my
"slightly" is the same as
pattern's "slightly." I assume
the fabric is to be stretched
until the purl stitches are
visible, but how far? For
this pattern, a reasonable
"slightly" will give 5 stitches
per inch, slightly stretched.

Practice knit and purl stitches with ribbing—
the most common knit-purl pattern.

This project will give you practice with the most common knit-purl pattern—ribbing. Ribbing creates a thick stretchy fabric, based on alternating stacks of knit and purl stitches. The elasticity of ribbing makes it ideal for close-fitting parts of garments, such as cuffs. This sampler has the two most commonly used ribbing variations, double (2×2) and single (1×1). Ribbing patterns are named by the number of knit and purl stitches involved—2×2 ribbing alternates 2 knit stitches with 2 purl stitches; 1×1 ribbing alternates 1 knit stitch with 1 purl stitch. There are numerous variants of ribbing, including uneven combinations of knits and purls (such as 3×2 ribbing) and ribbings formed from stacks of other stitch combinations (for example, garter rib, mistake rib, cable rib, and twisted rib, among others.)

Because ribbing has a balance of knit and purl stitches, it is reversible and the edges won't curl. However, a 4-stitch garter-stitch border is worked at each side of this sampler to set off the ribbing (and to provide experience reading your knitting in different stitches).

PROJECT INSTRUCTIONS

NOTE Markers are used to separate the border stitches and the two rib patterns. Slip markers as you come to them.

 TRANSLATION To slip a marker, simply move it from the left needle to the right needle as you come to it.

Using the long-tail method, CO 48 st.

TRANSLATION "CO" means "cast on." In this case, cast on 48 stitches using the long-tail method.

WHY? The long-tail cast-on (see page 38) is a very common one, useful for most purposes, and can be used when no other cast-on method is specified in a pattern.

READ YOUR KNITTING Note that the side of the fabric that faces you as you work this cast-on is smoother than the other side. Often designers will want the first row worked after a long-tail cast-on to be the wrong side of a finished product for this reason. As you begin the first row after casting on with the long-tail method, the location of the yarn tail signals whether you're looking at the right or

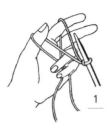

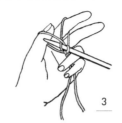

LONG-TAIL CAST-ON
Leaving a long tail (about ½" (1.3 cm) for each stitch to be cast on), make a slipknot and place it on the right needle. Place the thumb and index finger of your left hand between the

yarn ends so that the working yarn is around your index finger and the tail end is around your thumb, and secure the yarn ends with your other fingers. Hold your palm upward to make a V of

yarn **(FIGURE 1)**. *Bring the needle up through the loop on your thumb **(FIGURE 2)**, catch the first strand around your index finger, and go back down through the loop on your thumb **(FIGURE 3)**. Drop

the loop off your thumb and, placing your thumb back into the V configuration, tighten the resulting stitch on the needle **(FIGURE 4)**. Repeat from * for the desired number of stitches.

wrong side, but this will vary depending on the pattern. In this project, the tail will be on the right-hand side as you begin a wrong-side row.

ROW 1 (SET-UP ROW) (WS) K4, pm, [k1, p1] 10 times, pm, [k2, p2] 5 times, pm, knit to end.

 TRANSLATION A set-up row contains instructions that set up the work for a pattern in subsequent rows. It usually contains instructions that are worked only once. The instruction "pm" means to place a ring stitch marker on the needle after the specified number of stitches.

+ With the wrong side facing, knit 4 stitches, then place a marker on the right needle to separate pattern sections of the row. Repeat the pattern of "knit one stitch, purl one stitch" 10 times total (20 stitches). Place another stitch marker on the right needle. Repeat the pattern of "knit two stitches, purl two stitches" 5 times total (20 stitches). Place another stitch marker on the right needle. Knit the last 4 stitches.

TIP In the first row, you are establishing the ribbing patterns. Work the first row of any pattern very carefully and go back and check your stitches before working the second row to prevent mistakes. If your stitch count doesn't come out correctly, find the mistake, tink (see page 45) back to it, and rework the stitches as needed.

ROW 2 Knit to first marker, [k2, p2] 5 times, [k1, p1] 10 times, knit to end.

READ YOUR KNITTING The first 4 and last 4 stitches of each row are knitted, forming the pattern called garter stitch. The 2×2 and 1×1 ribbing patterns will be formed between the markers. The markers have a role similar to yellow caution lights when you are driving—they signal you to be alert for a change; in this case, a change in stitch pattern.

TIP The second and third markers are not mentioned in this row—it's up to you to know to slip them to the right needle as you come to them.

ROW 3 Keeping first and last 4 sts in garter st, work rib patts as established between markers.

> **READ YOUR KNITTING** The phrase "continue in pattern as established" is a common instruction. Once the pattern is established, instead of counting knits and purls as you work, you can tell which stitch to make next by seeing the stitch in the previous row. A stitch that was knitted in one row will appear as a purl in the following row. Verify this for yourself by looking at the reverse side of a knit stitch you just made and seeing that it will appear as a purl stitch on the opposite side. In ribbing, you knit the stitches that appear as knit stitches as they face you and you purl the purl stitches as they face you.

Rep Row 3 until piece measures 3" (7.5 cm) from beg, or desired length.

> **TRANSLATION** Repeat the instructions for Row 3 until the piece measures 3" (7.5 cm). Instructions will often tell you how to measure your piece. In this case, measure from the beginning (beg) or cast-on edge. Always measure up to but not including the loops on the needle.

> **WHY?** The length of this piece isn't important because it won't be anything more than a sample swatch. I suggest you work this ribbing until you feel comfortable working the pattern by reading your knitting and are happy with how your fabric looks and feels—not too uneven or sloppy. If you haven't made any mistakes, or if you can fix the ones that you do make, you've worked enough ribbing.

BO in patt.

> **TRANSLATION** "BO" means "bind off." "BO in patt" means to continue the established pattern as you bind off the stitches. In this case, you'll bind off in garter stitch and two ribbing patterns. When you come to a knit or purl stitch on the left needle, work it as you would in the underlying pattern. Pass the worked stitches over and off the right needle to bind off as usual.

> **WHY?** If you bind off your ribbing using all knit stitches, you will add a glaring inconsistency to the fabric. The chain of bound-off stitches will be visible across the right side of the work. By binding off in pattern, you will have a neat last row of ribbing and a nice chain across the top. Since you are just working this piece as an exercise, try binding off part of the ribbing section using all knit stitches, then binding off the rest in rib pattern to see the difference.

Weave in ends.

> **WHY?** Weaving in the ends gives a clean finish and keeps the ends from raveling. See page 29 for instruction on how to weave in ends.

Block lightly.

> **TRANSLATION** Blocking is a finishing technique using moisture and/or heat to relax the yarn, set the stitches, and improve appearance of the fabric. See page 31 for blocking advice.

> **TIP** Do not over-block ribbing, or it will lose its characteristic elasticity. Never stretch or press ribbing with a steam iron. When I blocked my sample, I stretched the garter-stitch borders vertically to match the length of the ribbing and I ever-so-slightly stretched the ribbing sideways to even up the piece.

Checkerboard Square

FINISHED SIZE

About 8" (20.5 cm) wide
and 8" (20.5 cm) long.

MATERIALS

+ Worsted-weight yarn
(#4 Medium).

SHOWN HERE Cascade 220 Wool
(100% wool; 220 yards
[201 meters]/100 grams):
#7829 red.

+ Size U.S. 7 (4.5 mm) needles
or size needed to obtain gauge
(I used size 8 [5 mm] needles
because I knit tightly).

+ 5 stitch markers.

+ 1 split-ring marker or
coil-less safety pin (in a pinch,
use paper clips for markers).

+ Tapestry needle.

+ Pins for blocking.

GAUGE

20 stitches and 28 rows = 4"
(10 cm); 5 stitches and 7 rows
= 1" (2.5 cm) in stockinette
stitch.

Learn to use stitch markers to keep track of different stitch patterns.

This square has alternating blocks of stockinette stitch and seed stitch and is bordered on all four sides with seed stitch.

PROJECT INSTRUCTIONS

CO 40 sts using the long-tail method.

🔄 **TRANSLATION** Cast on 40 stitches using the long-tail method (see page 38).

❓ **WHY?** We want a finished width of 8" (20.5 cm). Our gauge is 5 stitches per inch: 8" × 5 stitches/inch = 40 stitches.

📖 **READ YOUR KNITTING** Note that as you turn the work to start Row 1, the tail left over from the long-tail cast-on will be on the right-hand side. This indicates that, for this project, you are facing the right side (abbreviated RS) of your work. In this pattern, the right-side rows will be the odd-numbered rows. Remember that in stockinette stitch, stitches are always knitted on right-side rows and purled on wrong-side (abbreviated WS) rows.

💡 **TIP** Designers will sometimes designate the first row worked after a long-tail cast-on to be a wrong-side row so that the smoother side of the cast-on will appear on the right side of the knitting.

ROWS 1, 3, AND 5 *K1, p1; rep from * across.

ROWS 2, 4, AND 6 *P1, k1; rep from * across.

❓ **WHY?** Seed stitch is a knit-one-purl-one pattern (a 2-stitch repeat) with the knits and purls alternating every other row. These 6 rows form the bottom border.

💡 **TIP** In the first row, you'll establish the seed-stitch pattern. Work the first row of any pattern very carefully and check your stitches before working the second row to prevent mistakes. Because you cast on an even number of stitches and started Row 1 with a knit stitch, the last stitch of the row should be a purl stitch.

📖 **READ YOUR KNITTING** Once the pattern is established, instead of counting "knit one, purl one" as you work, you can tell which stitch to make next by seeing the stitch in the previous row. A stitch that was knitted in one row will appear as a purl in the following row. In seed stitch, you'll knit the stitches that appear as purl stitches as they face you, and you'll purl the knit stitches as they face you.

Place markers at the boundaries between stitch patterns.

ROW 7 (BEGIN CHECKERBOARD PATTERN) (RS) [K1, p1] 2 times, *k8, [k1, p1] 4 times; rep from * once more, [k1, p1] 2 times.

TRANSLATION This row begins the checkerboard pattern and is a right-side (RS) row. The brackets tell you to repeat a series of maneuvers a specific number of times. For this row, you'll repeat the "k1, p1" sequence 2 times (4 stitches total), then knit 8 stitches, then work the "k1, p1" sequence 4 times (16 stitches total for the k8 and [k1, p1] 4 times), then repeat the sequence of the last 16 stitches (which begins at the *) once more, then work the "k1, p1" sequence 2 times.

WHY? To maintain the 4-stitch seed-stitch border, the first and last 4 stitches in each row will be in seed-stitch, which is indicated as "[k1, p1] 2 times." There are 4 checkerboard squares across the sample, each of which is 8 stitches wide: 4 squares × 8 stitches/square = 32 stitches. All together, these patterns account for all 40 stitches: 4 border stitches + 32 checkerboard stitches + 4 border stitches.

TIP Although the instructions don't specify to add markers, this is a great opportunity to practice their magic. As you work the row, place a stitch marker between each pattern change, one after the first 4 border stitches, then one after each block of 8 stitches for a total of 5 markers across

the row. I used a different color marker to set off each border, but this isn't necessary. The markers will be slipped (moved from the left to right needle) when you come to them as you work subsequent rows. Because this is the first row of a new pattern, stop and check that all stitches are correct. Then add a row marker on the right side of Row 7 to mark the first row of a pattern repeat. Use a split-ring marker, a coil-less safety pin, a piece of waste yarn woven into the row, or even a paper clip. Leave this marker in place until you finish the 12 rows of the checkerboard tier, then move it up to mark the first row of the next repeat or tier.

+ When a pattern states, "place marker" (pm), it usually means to add a stitch marker on the needle between stitches. A row marker is actually attached to a stitch or stitches. If a pattern calls for a row marker, it will usually say so specifically, for example, by saying "mark row." You can mark stitches and rows any time it will help you keep track of where you are.

ROW 8 [P1, k1] 2 times, *[p1, k1] 4 times, p8, rep from * once more, [p1, k1] 2 times.

WHY? This is a wrong-side row, so the stockinette stitches are purled and the seed stitches are worked opposite of the previous row.

TIP As you work, count the stitches between markers. You should always have 4 stitches before the first marker and 4 stitches after the last marker. There should always be 8 stitches between the other markers. If a stitch is inadvertently increased or decreased, it will be easier to spot in these short sections.

READ YOUR KNITTING Now that you understand the pattern and have added markers, you can work Row 8 by looking at your knitting instead of the pattern. Work the first 4 stitches (up to the first marker) in seed stitch. The first checkerboard you come to when the wrong side of the knitting is facing you will be in seed stitch, so continue in seed stitch to the next marker. The next checkerboard will be stockinette stitch—because this is a wrong-side row, you'll purl to the next marker. Repeat the seed stitch and stockinette checkerboards, then finish with the 4 seed stitch border stitches.

ROWS 9–18 Rep Rows 7 and 8 five more times.

WHY? Rows 7 through 18 complete a 12-row block or tier.

TIP To keep track of your completed rows, use a row counter or make checkmarks on a piece of paper. But if you forget to turn the counter or make a mark, it's good to know how to read the rows from your knitting itself.

READ YOUR KNITTING If you are comfortable with the pattern sequence now, you can knit without reference to the written instructions until the 12-row repeat is completed. Continue with the seed-stitch and stockinette blocks "as established" for 12 rows total. Just keep track of whether you are on a right- or wrong-side row, which you should be able to identify by the position of the yarn tail (on the right-hand edge on a right-side row) and by whether your stockinette checkerboard squares show knits (right side) or purls (wrong side).

+ How do you tell which row you are on? Remember that you marked the first row of a 12-row repeat. This counts as Row 1. Count each V from the marker to the needles, then count the loops on the needle as the last row worked. In this case, 12 rows have been worked. The last row worked (Row 12) is a wrong-side row (which you'll know because in this sample, all even-numbered rows are wrong-side rows).

ROW 19 [K1, p1] 2 times, *[k1, p1] 4 times, k8; rep from * once more, [k1, p1] 2 times.

Beginning with marker on Row 1, count each V up to the needles, then count the loops on your needle as the last row knitted. In this example, 12 rows have been knitted.

WHY? This row is the first row of the second tier of blocks. The first 4 and last 4 stitches are still in seed stitch, but the blocks are reversed, with the right-hand block now in seed stitch instead of stockinette.

TIP As you work the right-hand block in seed stitch, move the row marker into this row to mark it as the first row of the 12-row pattern repeat in this tier. Leave the stitch markers in place on the needle. Instead of counting stitches across the row, you can use your stitch markers to indicate when to switch between seed stitch and stockinette.

ROW 20 [P1, k1] 2 times, *p8, [p1, k1] 4 times; rep from * once more, [p1, k1] 2 times.

ROWS 21–30 Rep Rows 19 and 20 five more times.

WHY? These 10 rows complete the second tier of blocks.

ROWS 31–42 Rep Rows 7–18.

WHY? These rows form the third tier of blocks, which is identical to the first tier.

TIP As you start Row 31, move the row marker into a stitch in this row to mark the first row of the 12-row pattern repeat in this tier.

READ YOUR KNITTING By now, you can probably knit this tier of blocks without looking back at the stitch-by-stitch instructions for Rows 7–18.

ROWS 43–54 Rep Rows 19–30.

WHY? These rows form the fourth tier of blocks, which is identical to the second tier.

TIP As you start Row 43, move the row marker into a stitch in this row to mark the first row of the 12-row pattern repeat in this tier.

READ YOUR KNITTING You can probably knit this tier of blocks without looking back at the stitch-by-stitch instructions for Rows 19–30. The right-hand block will now be seed stitch. This tier is worked the same as the second tier.

ROWS 55–60 Rep Rows 1–6.

WHY? These 6 rows form the top seed stitch border.

TIP As you work Row 55—the first row of the top seed-stitch border—you can remove the stitch and row markers.

BO in patt.

WHY? If you bind off the seed-stitch pattern by knitting every stitch, you'll produce a glaring chain of bound-off stitches across the top of the right side of the work. However, if you bind off the last row of stitches in pattern (alternating a knit stitch with a purl stitch), the seed-stitch pattern will be maintained to the top.

Weave in ends. Block to measurements.

WHY? Blocking is another magic trick. Carefully applied moisture or heat cause the yarn to relax and the stitches to become more even. Minor inconsistencies in tension disappear. Your stitches look their best and precise measurements can be made. Before this piece is blocked, note that the seed-stitch sections seem a bit smaller than the stockinette sections. After blocking, all of the checkerboard squares will be the same size.

TIP Pin the moist piece to a flat surface so that it measures 8" (20.5 cm) square. If you worked with wool, there will be some flexibility in how much you can stretch the piece. See page 31 for tips on blocking.

Tinking Knit and Purl: Anticipating and Fixing Mistakes

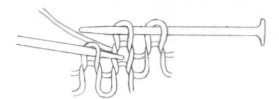

"Tink" is "knit" backwards, or un-knit. You will make mistakes in your knitting and tinking is knitting slang for undoing the knitting to fix the mistakes. The strategy is to tink back to the mistake, fix the mistake, then resume knitting from that point. Learning to tink is essential to your knitting sanity and peace of mind—mistakes can be fixed, knitting is not cast in stone, you are not a bad knitter. Tinking is not hard, but it does help to understand the concepts of stitch mount (see page 24).

To begin tinking, position your needles and yarn as they were when you finished the last stitch worked. (If you just finished a row, don't turn the work, but keep the needle with the stitches in your right hand.) Insert the left-hand needle from the front to the back into the stitch in the row below the last stitch worked (the one that was knitted or purled to form the last stitch). Once this stitch below is securely on the left needle (I like to secure it to the needle with my left index finger), slip the stitch above it off of the right needle and gently tug the working yarn to release the stitch above. Voila! One stitch tinked.

The only difference between tinking a knit or a purl stitch is the position of the working yarn. It will be easier (but not essential) if you have the working yarn in the position it was in when originally working the stitch being tinked.

Position the working yarn on the front when tinking a purl stitch and in the back when tinking a knit stitch.

If you have trouble finding the stitch in the row below, stretch the loop by pulling the working yarn upward to your left while pulling the finished fabric downward.

Knitting Math Pop Quiz

Q. If you use a thinner yarn with a gauge of six stitches per inch, how wide will the square end up? If you still want an 8" (20.5 cm) square, how many stitches would you need to cast on, and how would you revise the pattern to include those stitches?

A. At a gauge of 6 stitches per inch, the square will be 6.66" wide (40 stitches ÷ 6 stitches/inch = 6.66"). To make an 8" (20.5 cm) square at this gauge, you'd need to cast on 48 stitches (6 stitches/inch × 8" = 48 stitches). To include these stitches in the pattern, you could add one 8-stitch checkerboard square to make a total of 5 checkerboard squares instead of 4.

Working from a Chart

The Checkerboard Square chart, right, shows every stitch in this square, each represented by a single cell. Compare this chart to the one plotted on "knitter's" graph paper, which takes into account that stitches are not true squares—they are a little wider than they are tall. In this example, there are 5 stitches and 7 rows per inch of knitting. Charts on knitter's graph paper have the advantage of accurately representing the stitch and row relationship. The chart remains square, like the knitting itself. However, different gauges of knitting require different sizes of chart cells so this refinement is often not used in published patterns. You will most often find charts with square cells, resulting in distorted spatial representation—the Checkerboard Square chart is actually rectangular. Don't be confused by this. The rest of the charts in this book will have square cells, regardless of the gauge of the actual knitting.

Across each row, the chart is read in the same order as the stitches are worked, or "boustrophedonically," when the knitting is worked back and forth in rows. Boustrophedon is an ancient form of writing that is read right to left on one line and left to right on the next. It comes from Greek words that translate to "ox turning as a field is plowed." In other words, read the chart from right to left for right-side rows and from left to right for wrong-side rows.

For this chart, a blank cell indicates a stitch that is knitted on right-side rows and purled on wrong-side rows; a cell with a dot indicates a stitch that is purled on right-side rows and knitted on wrong-side rows. Chart symbols do not have universal definitions—charts in different publications may use different symbols. Therefore, every chart will be accompanied by a key that explains the meaning of each symbol. The symbol key for this chart is shown at right.

Charts are also labeled with row numbers. Typically, rows are numbered from the bottom to the top with

right-side rows labeled on the right-hand side of the chart (indicating that these rows are read from right to left) and wrong-

CHECKERBOARD SQUARE

side rows are labeled on the left-hand side of the chart (indicating that these rows are read from left to right). Sometimes the wrong-side row numbers are not shown, but you can infer them from preceding and subsequent right-side row numbers. Wrong-side row numbers are not shown on the rest of the charts in this book.

Not all charts follow these conventions—some charts, such as those for knitting socks in the round from the cuff to the toe, are designed to be read from the top to the bottom. I once knitted a Christmas stocking with a picture of Santa Claus on the leg. The chart showed Santa right side up, with Row 1 at the top of the chart. I had to turn the chart upside down to orient it in the same direction as the rows were worked.

Whether you knit from a chart or row-by-row instructions, the result is exactly the same. Verify this for yourself by

re-reading a few of the row-by-row instructions while looking at the chart for the same rows. As you gain experience, you may develop a preference for one or the other, but it's a good idea to be comfortable with both.

CHART KEY

☐ k on RS; p on WS

☐• p on RS; k on WS

CHECKERBOARD SQUARE PLOTTED ON KNITTER'S GRAPH PAPER

Diamond Peaks Square

FINISHED SIZE

About 8" (20.5 cm) wide
and 8" (20.5 cm) long.

MATERIALS

+ Worsted-weight yarn
(#4 Medium).

SHOWN HERE Cascade 220 Wool
(100% wool; 220 yards
[201 meters]/100 grams):
#7829 red.

+ Size U.S. 7 (4.5 mm) needles
or size needed to obtain gauge
(I used size 8 [5 mm] needles
because I knit tightly).

+ Tapestry needle.

+ Pins for blocking.

GAUGE

20 stitches and 28 rows = 4"
(10 cm); 5 stitches and 7 rows
= 1" (2.5 cm) in Diamond
Peaks Pattern.

In this symmetrical square, purl-stitch zigzags turn into seed-stitch diamonds that turn back into purl-stitch zigzags.

This square has a garter-stitch border and a design of purl-stitch zigzags against a stockinette-stitch background. The zigzags get closer together toward the center of the square where they turn into seed-stitch diamonds. Notice that very few of the rows are the same. If the pattern were written out in words, almost every row would need to be written separately. This is hard to write, hard to read, and prone to error. This type of pattern is more easily conveyed in a chart.

PROJECT INSTRUCTIONS

CO 41 sts using long-tail method.

? WHY? We want the piece to measure 8" (20.5 cm) wide and we have a gauge of 5 stitches per inch: 8" × 5 stitches/inch = 40 stitches. But for this pattern, which is symmetrical around a center stitch, we need an odd number of stitches. The additional single stitch won't affect the size significantly.

READ YOUR KNITTING Note that as you turn the work to start Row 1, the tail left over from the long-tail cast-on will be on the right-hand side of the piece. This is your indicator that, for this project, you are facing the right side of your work. In this pattern, right-side rows will be the odd-numbered rows.

Follow the Diamonds Peaks chart for Rows 1–61.

TIP To make it easier to keep your place, place a sticky note above the row you are on. This will help you see how the stitches on the needles relate to the rows already worked. (If you use a magnetic easel to hold your pattern, use one of the magnetic rulers for this purpose.)

+ Be sure to check the key for the chart symbols (see page 51). In this chart, a blank cell indicates a stitch to be knitted on right-side (odd-numbered) rows and purled on wrong-side (even-numbered) rows. A cell with a dot indicates a stitch to be purled on right-side (odd-numbered) rows and knitted on wrong-side (even-numbered) rows.

+ To help keep track of the different stitch patterns across a row beginning with Row 5, place a marker after the first 4 stitches and before the last 4 stitches to separate the garter stitch borders from the center pattern.

READ YOUR KNITTING As you work Rows 8–11, look at the previous row to see what stitch comes next. For example, on Row 8, you need to create a purl bump on the right side of the work both before and after each purl bump created in Row 7 to create the diagonal lines. Uh-oh—this is a wrong-side (even-numbered) row so most stitches will be purl bumps in stockinette stitch! In this case, you will *knit* the stitches that will form purl bumps on the opposite side. Then on the next row (Row 9), you will be back to purling the bumps. It becomes harder to read your knitting on subsequent rows when stitches from more than one of the zigzags are in the same row, as in Row 22.

TIP Reading the stitches is harder when looking at the wrong side of the piece because there are so many purl bumps. Before you start each right-side row, take a look at the right-side results of the last wrong-side row to make sure the sequence of bumps matches the pattern.

BO knitwise.

TRANSLATION The word "knitwise" means to use knit stitches as opposed to purl stitches ("purlwise") or another pattern.

TIP In this project, the diamond peaks pattern contains an odd number of rows, but the garter-stitch border contains an even number of rows. As a result, you will end up binding off on a wrong-side row. But because both right-side and wrong-side rows are knitted in the border, you will bind off while knitting (called "knitwise").

Weave in ends. Block to measurements.

TIP The garter-stitch border will be shorter than the center panel. You can even this out in blocking by stretching the piece evenly in all directions and pinning it out to an 8" (20.5 cm) square.

Unintentional Yarnovers and Dropped Stitches

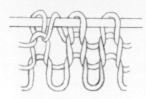

A yarnover is formed if the yarn travels over the right-hand needle when switching positions between knit and purl stitches. Here, there are four loops on the needle but only 3 stitches in the row below.

It's not uncommon for a yarnover to appear "out of nowhere" when changing from knit to purl stitches in a row of knitting. When switching between knits and purls, the working yarn must be brought from the back of the work (where it is used for a knit stitch) to the front of the work (where it is used for a purl stitch) or vice versa. If you mistakenly bring the yarn over the top of the right needle instead of between the needles, an extra loop will result on the needle. This loop is not connected to a stitch in the row below and is called a "yarnover."

A similar maneuver is done intentionally in shaping and lace knitting and will be used in later chapters. In the knit-and-purl patterns in this chapter, you don't want any yarnovers. By the way, unintentional yarnovers are often mismounted, as shown in the illustration here. If you inadvertently create a yarnover, simply drop the loop off the needle when you come to it on the next row of knitting.

Another common problem is dropped stitches. When stitches unintentionally slip off the needle (and they will from time to time), do not panic. Without putting any stress on the dropped stitches, calmly reinsert the needle into them, grabbing them however you can. Once the stitches are safely on the needle, you can correct the stitch mount as necessary. If you can't grab the stitch before it starts to run down, grab the stitch in the row below, tink back to that stitch, then continue as usual.

DIAMOND PEAKS

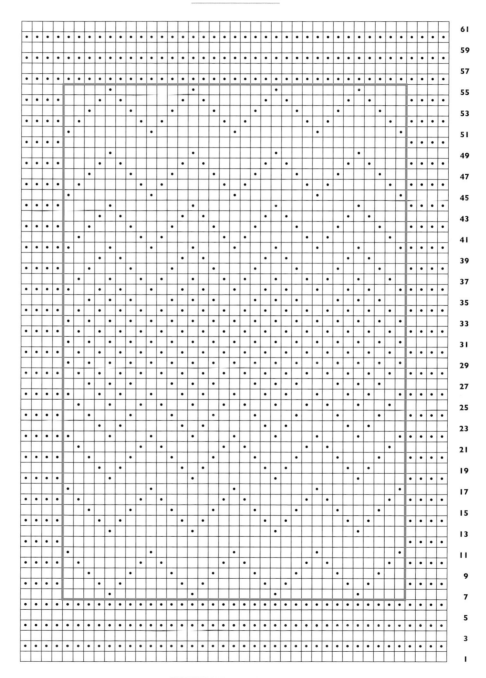

CHART KEY

☐ k on RS; p on WS

• p on RS; k on WS

Working from an Abbreviated Chart

Many patterns provide an abbreviated chart that shows just the pattern repeat instead of every stitch. This saves space and helps the knitter see the pattern repetition, which makes it easier to memorize stitch sequences. But first you need to understand how to read and work with these minimal charts.

Just like a complete chart, this type of chart is typically read from the bottom up. The difference is that the groups of stitches that form a pattern repeat are shown just once. The repeating element(s) are typically outlined in red for clarity. In the abbreviated chart for the Diamond Peaks Square, note that the garter-stitch borders are not included. Simple named patterns (such as

seed stitch, garter stitch, and stockinette stitch) may not be charted because it is assumed that the knitter can follow these patterns from memory, once they've been established in the project.

Compare this chart to the full chart on page 51, in which there are four repeats of the same 8-stitch pattern across each row. Because the last stitch of one peak is the first stitch of the next peak, we need to add 1 additional stitch at the end of the sequence to make the last repetition complete. This extra (balancing) stitch appears outside the red pattern repeat box. The instructions for knitting the sample square based on the abbreviated chart follow.

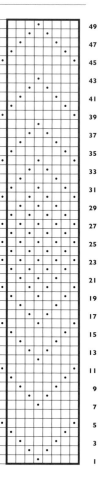

CO 41 sts using long-tail method.

ROWS 1–6 Knit across.

ROWS 7–55 K4, work Rows 1–49 of chart across next 33 sts, end k4.

🔄 **TRANSLATION** The word "end . . ." in instructions is used to signal a set of stitches to be worked at the end of the row that is different from the pattern worked previously in the row. This is usually because there are too few stitches to complete a repeat or because a border pattern is being used. The stitches described after the word "end" are worked just once at the end of the row.

💡 **TIP** One of the advantages of abbreviated charts is that it is easier to recognize and memorize a pattern repetition. Look at Row 1 of the abbreviated chart. This is a right-side row, so the repeating section of the chart shows the following sequence: k4, p1, k3. As you continue this across the row, the sequence will be k4, p1, k3, k4, p1, k3, k4, p1, k3, etc. Notice that after the first k4, you will actually be working p1, k7 (adding the k3 and k4), until the last repeat when you will end p1, k4. Similarly, on Row 3 of the chart, after the first k2, you will actually work p1, k3 across, ending p1, k2. Taking a few moments to analyze a chart at the beginning of a new row can make the pattern easier and faster to work.

+ A potential confusion here is that the chart row numbers no longer match the actual row numbers of your knitting. You will be working Row 1 of the chart on the 7th row of your knitting. To keep this straight, you can add a row marker to your knitting to indicate Row 1 of the pattern. You can also make notes on the pattern (or a photocopy of the pattern) to remind yourself of this discrepancy.

+ Because the top half of the pattern in this square is the mirror image of the bottom half, this chart could be abbreviated even further by eliminating Rows 26–49. The instructions for project Rows 7–55 would then read:

ROWS 7–31 K4, work Rows 1–25 of chart across next 33 st, end k4.

ROWS 32–55 K4, work Rows 24–1 of chart across next 33 sts (i.e., work Row 24 of chart for row 32 of the square, then work Row 25 of chart for row 33 of the square, and so on), end k4.

ROWS 56–61 Rep Rows 1–6.

BO knitwise. Weave in ends. Block to measurements.

Maple Leaf Square

FINISHED SIZE

About 8" (20.5 cm) wide
and 8" (20.5 cm) long.

MATERIALS

+ Worsted-weight yarn
(#4 Medium).

SHOWN HERE Cascade 220 Wool
(100% wool; 220 yards
[201 meters]/100 grams):
#7829 red.

+ Size U.S. 7 (4.5 mm) needles
or size needed to obtain gauge.

+ Tapestry needle.

+ Pins for blocking.

GAUGE

20 stitches and 28 rows = 4"
(10 cm); 5 stitches and 7 rows
= 1" (2.5 cm) in stockinette
stitch.

Although this leaf motif looks symmetrical, the right and left sides are slightly different, and the project is best worked from a chart.

This maple leaf is worked in purl stitches against a stockinette-stitch background bordered with seed stitch. Although the leaf is divided into two halves by a vertical line of purl stitches, the halves are not identical and cannot be worked from memory. Instead, row-by-row instructions must be followed, either written out or plotted on a chart. The seed-stitch border is not charted—it is up to you to figure out and keep track of the border stitch pattern.

PROJECT INSTRUCTIONS

CO 41 sts.

TRANSLATION Cast on 41 stitches. Because the instructions don't specify a cast-on method, it is a matter of "knitter's choice." Use the cast-on of your choice.

WHY? We want the piece to measure 8" (20.5 cm) wide and we have a gauge of 5 stitches per inch: 8" × 5 stitches/inch = 40 stitches. But for this pattern, we need an odd number of stitches. The additional single stitch won't affect the size significantly.

ROWS 1-4 Work in seed st.

ROWS 5-52 Keeping first and last 3 sts in seed st as established, work Rows 1–48 of Maple Leaf chart across center 35 sts.

WHY? This square has a 3-stitch border because the center panel is 35 stitches wide. Only 6 more stitches are needed to get to the 41 needed for the desired 8" (20.5 cm) width.

READ YOUR KNITTING Once the seed-stitch pattern is established, you can determine how to work the border seed stitches in subsequent rows by examining the stitches in the row below.

TIP The seed-stitch borders are not shown on the chart. Many published project charts omit simple and repetitive border stitches. Read the general instructions for the pattern and analyze the chart before you begin so you can make a plan for adding the border. You might add stitch markers to remind you of the border stitches.

+ Use a sticky note or magnetic easel to keep your place in the chart and to indicate where you are in the row in relation to the previous row. For example, on right-side Row 7 of the chart, you can count across k5, p9, k3, p1. The "p1" corresponds to the center stitch of the chart, which shows as a purl bump produced by a knit stitch worked in wrong-side Row 6. If you find that your stitches don't line up this way, you can be sure that you've made a mistake. Remember, a cell with a dot indicates a stitch that is purled on the right side but knitted on the wrong side. Take a moment at the beginning of a row to verify which side you're on by looking for the location of the cast-on tail. It sometimes helps to place a row marker on the right side of the piece.

+ I find it easiest to keep my place when working an irregular chart if I place the chart directly behind the knitting—on a table or on my lap— so I can glance easily back and forth between the needles and the chart. If I only need to refer to a chart once at the beginning of a row, I set it to the side instead.

+ When I knitted this sample, I forgot to move my sticky note up a row on the chart after knitting Row 40. I then repeated Row 40 for the next right-side row. I discovered the mistake when I moved the sticky note to start Row 41 and, by reading my knitting, noticed that I was ready for a wrong-side row! I tinked the second (incorrect) Row 40 and got back on track.

ROWS 53–56 Work in seed st.

BO in patt. Weave in ends. Block to measurements.

MAPLE LEAF

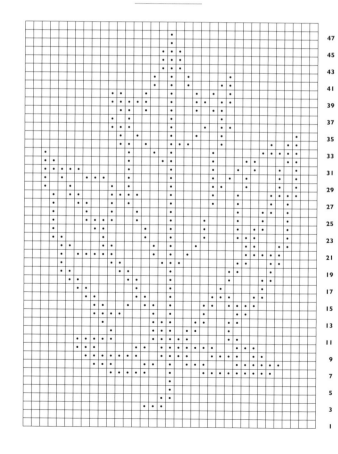

CHART KEY

☐ k on RS; p on WS

▪ p on RS; k on WS

Leaf Pillows

Any of the practice squares can be appliquéd onto a pillow. Purchase a pillow with a coordinating cover—the pillows shown here were covered with a machine-knitted fabric.

FINISHED SIZE

Each appliqué measures about 8" (20 cm) square on an 18" (45.5 cm) pillow.

MATERIALS

+ Worsted-weight (#4 Medium) yarn.
SHOWN HERE Berroco Comfort (50% nylon, 50% acrylic; 210 yards [193 meters]/100 grams): #9730 teaberry (red) and #9721 spring (light olive), 1 ball for each appliqué.

+ Size 8 (5 mm) needles or size needed to obtain gauge.

+ Tapestry needle.

+ A few yards (meters) of brown yarn for joining appliqué.

+ Two 18" (45.5 cm) square pillows.

GAUGE

20 stitches and 28 rows = 4" (10 cm); 5 stitches and 7 rows = 1" (2.5 cm) in stockinette stitch.

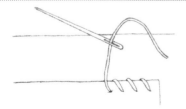

WHIPSTITCH APPLIQUÉ Thread yarn on a tapestry needle. Working from right to left, *insert needle through both layers from back to front close to the boundary between the two. Repeat from *, keeping even tension on the seaming yarn.

PROJECT INSTRUCTIONS

Appliqué Squares

With red, follow the instructions for the Maple Leaf Square on page 54. With light olive, follow the instructions for the Oak Leaf Square on page 58.

Assembly

Pin one appliqué to the center of each pillow. With brown threaded on a tapestry needle, use a whipstitch (shown at left) to appliqué the squares to the pillow background, being careful not to pierce the pillow form underneath.

Extra Credit
Oak Leaf Square

FINISHED SIZE

About 8" (20.5 cm) wide
and 8" (20.5 cm) long.

MATERIALS

+ Worsted-weight yarn
(#4 Medium).

SHOWN HERE Cascade 220
Wool (100% wool; 220 yards
[201 meters]/100 grams):
#7829 red.

+ Size U.S. 7 (4.5 mm)
needles or size needed
to obtain gauge.

+ Tapestry needle.

+ Pins for blocking.

GAUGE

20 stitches and 28 rows =
4" (10 cm); 5 stitches
and 7 rows = 1" (2.5 cm)
in stockinette stitch.

A chart is indispensible when working irregular patterns with unpredictable stitch sequences.

This leaf is worked in stockinette stitch against a reverse-stockinette background and bordered with seed stitch. The central vein is created with purl stitches, but the shape is highly irregular, so the sequence of stitches is unpredictable. Although some tricks are given to help manage the knitting, this type of pattern requires careful counting. Working from a chart will allow you to see the relationship of the stitches between rows.

PROJECT INSTRUCTIONS

CO 40 sts using cable cast-on method.

WHY? The cable cast-on (see page 60) produces a strong and stretchy edge. It is worked with just the working yarn end (not two ends, as in the long-tail method), so it can be used to cast on stitches mid-project, such as at the end of a row where you have only one strand of yarn to work with (more on this in the Knitting in Rounds chapter). For this sample, the cable method is used to illustrate that the yarn tail isn't always on the same edge of your work as you begin.

READ YOUR KNITTING When you turn the work to start Row 1, the tail left over from the cable cast-on will be on the left-hand side of the knitting (when you used a long-tail cast-on, the tail was on the right-hand side). In this pattern, the tail will be on the left-hand side of the work for right-side rows, which will be odd-numbered rows. In stockinette stitch, stitches are knitted on right-side rows and purled on wrong-side rows. The reverse stockinette-stitch background in this square (surprise!) reverses this, so that stitches are purled on right-side rows and knitted on wrong-side rows.

Work Rows 1–56 of Oak Leaf chart.

TIP Be sure to check this chart's specific key for the chart symbols. This chart uses colors to represent stitch patterns (stockinette, reverse stockinette, and seed stitch) instead of representing individual stitches. It is up to the knitter to figure out what each stitch should be, based on the stitch pattern indicated. Since the stitch patterns used are familiar and easy, this shouldn't be too difficult.

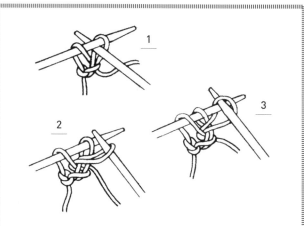

CABLE CAST-ON If there are no stitches on the needles, make a slipknot of working yarn and place it on the left needle. Use the Knitted method (below) to cast on one more stitch—2 stitches on needle. *Insert the right needle between the first 2 stitches on the left needle **(FIGURE 1)**, wrap the yarn around the needle as if to knit, draw yarn through **(FIGURE 2)**, and place the new loop on the left needle **(FIGURE 3)** to form a new stitch. Repeat from *, always working between the first 2 stitches on the left needle.

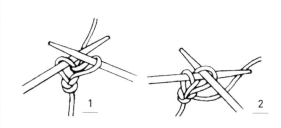

KNITTED CAST-ON Make a slipknot of working yarn and place it on the left needle. *Use the right needle to knit the first stitch (or slipknot) on the left needle **(FIGURE 1)** and place the new loop onto the left needle **(FIGURE 2)** to form a new stitch. Repeat from *, always working into the last stitch made.

+ In this chart, both the gray color and the dots indicate stitches that are purled on right-side rows and knitted on wrong-side rows. This is done to make the vein stitches stand out against the stockinette leaf stitches in the chart and because the vein stitches are worked as individual stitches instead of as entire areas of a stitch pattern.

+ The first 4 rows are seed stitch, so work k1, p1, across Row 1, then knit the purls and purl the knits across the next 3 rows. Row 5, a right-side row, begins with 3 seed stitches followed by reverse stockinette (purl on right side) to the last 4 stitches, which are worked as 1 stitch in stockinette (knit on right-side rows) followed by 3 stitches in seed stitch. For seed stitch, purl the knits of the previous row and knit the purls of the previous row. In this case, work the stitches as p1, k1, p1.

READ YOUR KNITTING As you work the chart from left to right for Row 6, note that the switch from reverse stockinette to stockinette (knitting to purling on a wrong-side row) occurs 1 stitch past the switch on the previous row, and then it switches back to reverse stockinette after 2 purl stitches. The following row (Row 7) is worked from right to left and the switch occurs 5 stitches *before* the switch on the previous row. These 5 stitches are easier to count than the 26 purl stitches that precede them.

TIP It's a good idea to photocopy a chart that you can mark with personal notes and comments. For this pattern, it would be helpful to note the numbers of stitches in the rows when the number isn't immediately obvious. The chart shows counts added to Row 19 (worked right to left) to show that there are 8 reverse stockinette stitches followed by 11 stockinette stitches before 2 more reverse stockinette stitches for the vein.

BO in patt. Weave in ends. Block to measurements.

OAK LEAF SQUARE

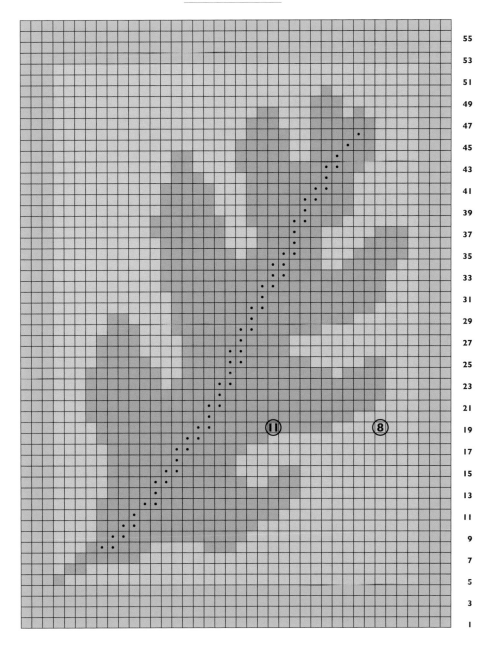

CHART KEY

- seed stitch
- stockinette stitch
- reverse stockinette stitch

- • p on RS; k on WS
- (8) number of stitches worked the same

BORDERED GARTER SQUARE, PAGE 74

03

GET IN SHAPE!
BASIC SHAPING TECHNIQUES

Knitted pieces come in all shapes. Two-dimensional flat pieces can be round, square, or almost any other complex shape (think raglan or cap sleeves). Three-dimensional knitting can form tubes that are open, closed at one or both ends, or bent (think socks that are closed at one end and bend at the heel). How is shaping accomplished? It is the result of just four basic methods and innumerable variations on those methods.

This chapter focuses on two ways to shape a piece of knitting—by changing the number of stitches or by changing direction. The first sample square, which is the easiest, uses one type of increase and one type of decrease to produce shape. Subsequent samples include more types of increases and decreases and vary their placement within the rows of knitting. Instructions for the increases and decreases are given along the way in this book, although in many published patterns, all the techniques may be grouped into a glossary at the end. Keep in mind that the names for increases and decreases are not necessarily standard—always check the instructions to make sure you're using the correct technique.

There are numerous ways to add and remove stitches in knitting, each with its own look. Depending on the method used and where it is placed in a row, the result can be quite evident or nearly invisible. For some projects, increases and decreases are used as design elements and are intended to be visible, following the "form follows function" architectural design principle. Think of a full-fashioned sweater where the decreases for the armhole and neck are worked a few stitches away from the edges and are fully visible, or a V-neck sweater with a perfect miter around a single vertical stitch at the base of the V. Think of a hat in which the decreases form a swirl design on top. For other projects, the increases and decreases are less visible. Think of an Icelandic-style yoke sweater that increases invisibly in circumference from the neck to the shoulders, or a sweater knitted in pieces where the shaping is worked at the edges and disappears into the seams.

Having a repertoire of increases and decreases is a knitter's equivalent of having a hammer and some screwdrivers; that is, having some of the most basic of tools. This section will expose you to the most frequently used increases and decreases.

When working any of the increases, you may find it difficult to maneuver your needle into the right place, especially if you're using inelastic yarn or if you are a tight knitter. If this is the case, try moving the working stitches to the tapered tip of the needle and wrapping the yarn loosely while working the stitch, then tighten the completed stitch on the main part of the needle.

Four Ways to Shape Your Knitting

1. CHANGING THE NUMBER OF STITCHES is the most common way to create shapes. You can add stitches by casting on stitches at either end of a row or by increasing stitches within a row. Similarly, you can remove stitches by binding off stitches at either end of a row or by decreasing stitches within a row. There are many, many ways to cast on, increase, bind off, and decrease stitches. The bottom line is that changing the number of stitches will change the width.

2. CHANGING THE GAUGE is a way to change the width without changing the number of stitches. One way to change gauge is to change the stitch pattern. Think of how ribbing can make the cuff of a mitten narrower than the stockinette-stitch hand, even if they are worked on the same number of stitches. Another way to change the gauge is to change the size of the needles.

3. KNITTING "SHORT-ROWS" is a way to change the length of part of a piece. Short-rows are simply rows that are knitted across only some of the stitches on the needle. The work is then turned and the knitting resumes in the other direction, making the piece longer where those stitches occur. Short-rows are used to shape the heel of a sock, the curve of a shawl collar, and pie-shaped wedges that can form a circle. Short-row techniques are difficult to visualize and won't be covered in this workbook.

4. ADDING ONTO THE SIDE OF A PIECE OF KNITTING makes a piece wider by knitting onto it in a different direction. One way to accomplish this is to "pick up and knit" stitches (create new stitches by looping the working yarn through the edge of the knitted piece). A less common method is to join two pieces together as they are knitted. This method, not covered in this workbook, is used to knit borders onto lace shawls or to create saddle shoulders of traditional ganseys, for example.

Tinking Increases and Decreases: Anticipating and Fixing Mistakes

Tinking, or un-knitting, increases and decreases is similar to un-knitting basic knit and purl stitches, but there are more loops to contend with, and sometimes these loops are twisted. When tinking a decrease, you still need to insert your left needle into the row below the row last worked, but you will be inserting your needle into more than one loop on that row below. Here are some situations you can encounter.

YARNOVER (YO) All you need to do is to drop the yarnover off of the right needle—there is no stitch in the row row below a yarnover so the stitch cannot ravel down.

MAKE-ONE INCREASE (M1, M1R, M1L, OR M1P) This type of increase creates a stitch from the horizontal strand between 2 existing stitches. To tink this type of increase, simply drop the stitch off the right needle and let the strand resume its place in the row below.

KNIT 2 TOGETHER (K2TOG) Insert the left needle tip from front to back into both loops of the decrease in the row below the row last worked, slide the right needle out of the stitch to be tinked, then tug on the working yarn to tink the stitch. Both loops of the decrease will end up on the left needle correctly mounted and reworked as needed.

SLIP, SLIP, KNIT (SSK) Insert the left needle tip from back to front into both loops of the decrease in the row below the row last worked, slide the right needle out of the stitch to be tinked, then tug on the working yarn to tink the stitch. The loops will be un-knitted, but they will be twisted on the left needle. Untwist the 2 stitches by inserting the right needle tip into each as if you were purling through the back loop (that is, from left to right and back to front). Once both stitches are on the right needle, slip them back to the left needle in their untwisted orientation.

Aunt Liz's and Aunt Nadine's Dishcloth Square

FINISHED SIZE

About 8" (20.5 cm) square, after blocking.

MATERIALS

+ Worsted-weight yarn (#4 Medium).

SHOWN HERE Cascade 220 Wool (100% wool; 220 yards [201 meters]/100 grams): #8229 blue.

+ Size U.S. 7 (4.5 mm) needles or size needed to obtain gauge.

+ Tapestry needle.

+ Pins for blocking.

GAUGE

20 stitches and 40 rows = 4" (10 cm); 5 stitches and 10 rows = 1" (2.5 cm) in garter stitch, unblocked.

To knit a square on the diagonal, begin with a few stitches, work increases at each edge to the desired width, then work decreases at each edge until just a few stitches remain.

This venerable pattern may look familiar to you. It makes a classic dishcloth when worked in simple cotton or a facecloth when worked in softer cotton chenille. I've named it for my Aunt Elizabeth and my best friend Dawn's Aunt Nadine, because both have made lots of them. The sample square is worked in wool, but you can substitute worsted-weight cotton if you want to make a dishcloth. Cotton chenille makes a wonderful fabric but is very frustrating to work with, even for experienced knitters (it is used in the Bordered Diagonal Garter Square on page 74).

Although this project forms a square, it is knitted on the diagonal, beginning with a small number of stitches at one corner and ending with a small number of stitches at the opposite corner. One stitch is increased every row by working a yarnover, a technique that forms intentional holes. In addition to functioning as increases, yarnovers are decorative and are the foundation of knitted lace. In this project, they serve both functions. The yarnovers are worked 2 stitches in from each edge to form an eyelet border. Once the piece is the desired width, decreases are worked to taper it back down to just a few stitches at the opposite corner. The tricky bit with this pattern is that the yarnovers have to be continued to maintain the decorative edge. But yarnovers add stitches and we want to eliminate stitches in the second half—what do we do? The answer is to decrease 2 stitches for each yarnover in the second half of the square, 1 to compensate for the yarnover and 1 to serve as an actual decrease. Because lace patterns are based on yarnovers paired with decreases, this project is a good introduction to lace knitting.

This square is worked in garter stitch, in which every row is knitted. Garter stitch has a different row gauge from stockinette stitch and we can take advantage of that to shape a diagonal square. If we tried to work this project in stockinette stitch, we would end up with an elongated diamond, not a square.

Before you begin, review how to make a yarnover and how to decrease stitches on page 69.

PROJECT INSTRUCTIONS

CO 4 sts.

🔄 **TRANSLATION** Cast on 4 stitches. No particular cast-on method is specified, so use the method of your choice.

❓ **WHY?** The number of stitches cast on includes 2 border stitches from each side.

ROW 1 (INC ROW) K2, yo, k to end.

🔄 **TRANSLATION** The words "inc row" alert you that the stitch count will change. This instruction often signals that the increase row will be referred to by name later in the pattern, so the designation helps you find the instructions again later.

❓ **WHY?** Each yarnover is worked 2 stitches in from the beginning of the row to form the border. Why didn't the instruction say "k2, yo, k2"? Because that would make this instruction work for only the first row that has 4 stitches; by saying "k to end," the same instructions can be reused for subsequent rows that have different stitch counts.

📖 **READ YOUR KNITTING** After working Row 1, there should be 5 stitches because the yarnover increased the stitch count by 1.

Repeat the inc row until the diagonal edge, measured along the inside of the yarnovers, measures 7½" (19 cm)—about 55 stitches and 25 garter ridges.

❓ **WHY?** In this case, we do not want to measure the length of our knitting from the needle down to the cast-on edge as usual, but along the diagonal edge because that is how the width or length of the square is measured. We want to end up with about an 8" (20.5 cm) square. There is a mathematical formula that will tell us how long the knitting needs to be to produce an 8" (20.5 cm) square on the diagonal, but that's more math than we need to finish this project. Simply measure along the inside of the yarnovers.

+ Because garter stitch looks the same on the right and wrong side, the same instructions will work for both sides of the knitting. By increasing 1 stitch at the beginning of every row, we alternate which side of the piece the increases are worked when we turn the work around between right- and wrong-side rows.

💡 **TIP** If you plan to use this square as a dishcloth, you can make it any size you want. Keep knitting until the square is half the finished size, then begin working the next instruction for the decrease row.

Note

Garter stitch has a different row gauge than stockinette stitch. When working stockinette stitch at 5 stitches per inch, the row gauge was 7 rows per inch. In garter stitch, however, there are 10 rows per inch. Why are the row gauges different? Visualize your knitting from the side, as in a cross-section. In stockinette stitch, each row is aligned nearly vertically against the next, like a closed window blind. In garter stitch, each row lies at an angle between the adjacent rows, more like a pleated window shade. The stitches are the same size in the two patterns, but some of the length in the garter stitches goes in the horizontal direction, making the resulting fabric shorter but thicker for the same number of rows. Every 2 rows form one horizontal garter ridge, so there will be 5 garter ridges for each inch.

NEXT ROW (DEC ROW) K1, k2tog, yo, k2tog, k to end.

🔄 **TRANSLATION** Knit the first stitch in the row, then make the first decrease by knitting 2 stitches together. Make a yarnover to continue the eyelet pattern, followed by a second decrease (also formed by knitting 2 stitches together) to counteract the yarnover and prevent the stitch count from increasing. Finish by knitting to the end of the row.

❓ **WHY?** The decrease row involves working k2tog decreases 2 times—once to decrease the stitch count by 1 and once to compensate for the yarnover. The first stitch is knitted to maintain the border.

Rep the dec row until 5 sts rem.

NEXT ROW K1, k2tog, yo, k2tog—4 sts rem.

❓ **WHY?** The "knit to end" instructions are omitted for this row because there are no stitches after the second k2tog.

BO. Weave in ends. Optional: block to desired measurements.

❓ **WHY?** If you have made a cotton dishcloth, blocking doesn't make much sense for something that's going to get wet and wrung out soon anyway. But blocking the square will teach you something useful about how cotton yarn behaves, so give it a try.

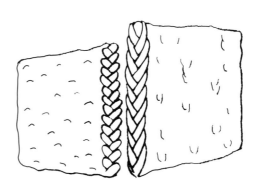

Stockinette stitches are predominantly vertical when viewed in cross section (right); garter stitches lay at an angle between horizontal and vertical, which causes there to be more rows per vertical inch of knitting (left).

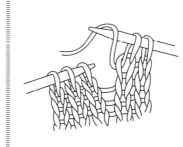

YARNOVER
In its simplest form, a yarnover is made by wrapping the yarn around the right needle from front to back to create 1 additional stitch.

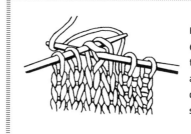

KNIT 2 TOGETHER (K2TOG) Knit 2 stitches together as if they were a single stitch—1 stitch decreased; decrease slants to the right.

Which Way is Up?

FINISHED SIZE

About 8" (20.5 cm) square,
after blocking.

MATERIALS

+ Worsted-weight yarn
(#4 Medium).

SHOWN HERE Cascade 220 Wool
(100% wool; 220 yards
[201 meters]/100 grams):
#8229 blue.

+ Size U.S. 7 (4.5 mm)
straight or circular needles, or
size needed to obtain gauge.

+ Tapestry needle.

+ Pins for blocking.

GAUGE

20 stitches and 40 rows = 4"
(10 cm); 5 stitches and 10 rows
= 1" (2.5 cm) in garter stitch,
unblocked.

This project demonstrates that, in garter stitch, two rows occupy the same width as one stitch of knitting.

This square is created from two rectangles that are knitted in different directions—90° apart. To accomplish this, we'll take advantage of the fact that in garter stitch, 2 rows occupy the same width as 1 stitch of knitting. We'll begin by knitting a strip that is half the desired width and the full desired length, then we'll bind off all but the last stitch, turn the work 90°, and pick up stitches along the side edge in preparation to resume knitting in a different direction. To facilitate picking up the stitches, we'll slip the first stitch of the odd-numbered rows to create a smooth chain edge that makes it easy to see exactly where to pick up stitches.

Instructions commonly call for picking up stitches to add a collar or neckband to a sweater or to add button and buttonhole bands to the front of a cardigan. In garter stitch, you'll pick up 1 stitch for every 2 rows of knitting (every garter "ridge"). Typically these patterns do not call for slipped edge stitches so you'll have to pay closer attention to reading your knitting to know where to pick up the stitches.

PROJECT INSTRUCTIONS

CO 21 sts.

 WHY? The first rectangle to be worked is 4" (10 cm) wide. At a gauge of 5 stitches per inch, that requires 20 stitches (4" × 5 stitches/inch = 20 stitches). An additional stitch is added for the slipped edge stitch.

First Rectangle

ROW 1 AND SUBSEQUENT ODD-NUMBERED ROWS IN FIRST RECTANGLE Sl 1 wyf, k to end.

 WHY? These instructions don't refer to right- and wrong-side rows because either side can be considered the right side.

 TIP Use the position of the cast-on yarn tail to indicate the odd or even rows. You may also want to place a row marker in the first row to mark the side you'll look at when working odd-numbered rows. Once the pattern of slipped stitches is established, you will be able to read the finished knitting itself.

ROW 2 AND ALL SUBSEQUENT EVEN-NUMBERED ROWS K all sts across.

Rep these 2 rows 37 more times, then rep Row 1 once more.

 WHY? We need to end up with 39 slipped stitches along the slipped selvedge and we need to end after an odd-numbered row so that, when binding off, the working yarn will be positioned at the slipped-stitch edge, ready for picking up stitches.

 READ YOUR KNITTING Instead of counting rows over and over, count the slipped edge stitches. Add another row marker after 20 rows or 30 rows. That way, you can count just the slipped stitches after the marker, a much smaller number. After completing an even-numbered row, there will be half as many slipped edge stitches as rows worked.

BO on an even-numbered row, leaving last st on right needle. Do not cut yarn.

Second Rectangle

Pick up and knit 39 sts along slipped st edge—40 sts total on right needle.

 TIP See page 73 for general instructions on how to pick up and knit. It's pretty easy to do on our piece because the slipped stitches are large and easy to see.

+ Be aware that "pick up" and "pick up and knit" can mean two different things. The term "pick up" can mean to simply lift loops from the knit piece onto the right needle tip without wrapping them with the working yarn—that will be done on a subsequent row. However, the terms aren't always used this way and they are sometimes

interchanged. "Pick up and knit" is the maneuver most commonly meant, but when reading a pattern, pay attention to where the working yarn is after the pick-up step to help you distinguish the difference between the two maneuvers.

Special Stitches

 WHY? Sometimes patterns will include abbreviations and instructions for less common stitches. Read these before starting to knit to make sure you understand them. Practice any new stitches on your gauge swatch.

SL 1 WYF Slip 1 stitch with yarn in front (see page 73).

 TRANSLATION Slip 1 stitch from the left needle to the right needle as if you were going to purl the stitch, but don't actually work it. The "with yarn in front" may seem odd when you are slipping the stitch in this pattern because it is always the first stitch of a row that is being slipped, but it is important for what happens to the next stitch. If the next stitch is a knit stitch (which it always is in this pattern), move the yarn to the back between the needles after slipping the first stitch, just as you would if you had just purled a stitch. In other words, don't knit that next stitch with the yarn still in the front.

Work garter st for 39 more rows.

 WHY? The picked-up stitches count as the first row of the 40 rows needed to complete the 4" (10 cm) rectangular half of the square. There is no need to slip stitches at the beginning of rows because no stitches will be picked up from this second rectangle.

READ YOUR KNITTING Notice that the chain of slipped stitches makes a lovely rib pattern. Usually the stitches through which other stitches are picked up are hidden on the wrong side, like a seam allowance. However, in this case they are also decorative. I prefer to think of this chain rib as being on the right side of the piece.

BO. Weave in ends. Block lightly if desired.

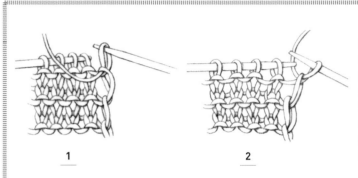

SLIP 1 WITH YARN IN FRONT (SL 1 WYF) Holding the yarn in front of the needles, insert the right needle tip into the first stitch on the left needle as if you were going to purl this stitch, then slip this stitch onto the right needle without working it **(FIGURE 1)**, then bring the working yarn to the back between the needles in preparation to knit the next stitch **(FIGURE 2)**.

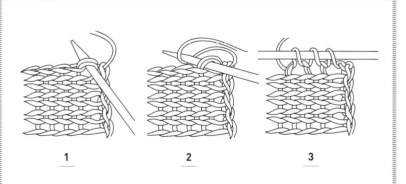

PICK UP AND KNIT Working from right to left, *insert the needle tip under the selvedge stitch from front to back **(FIGURE 1)**, wrap the yarn around the needle as if to knit **(FIGURE 2)**, and pull a loop through. Repeat from * for the desired number of stitches **(FIGURE 3)**.

The first half of the square is worked in one direction and the second half is worked 90° to the first. Arrows show the knitting direction. The photo on page 70 shows the "wrong" side of the knitting.

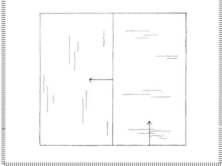

Bordered Diagonal Garter Square

Clockwise from upper left: fingering weight, worsted weight, heavy worsted weight, and chunky weight.

This project introduces another type of increase and decrease and gives you practice reading instructions for different yarns at different gauges.

FINISHED SIZE

About 8" (20.5 cm) square, after blocking.

NOTE The instructions are given first for fingering-weight yarn, followed by instructions in parentheses for worsted-weight, heavy worsted-weight, and chunky-weight yarn. When only one number is given, it applies to all yarn weights.

TIP To keep this straight, try highlighting, circling, or underlining the numbers that apply to your chosen yarn weight.

+ You might want to make a photocopy for personal use and highlight the appropriate numbers in the copy, especially if you plan to try this project in more than one yarn. Or write out the instructions just for your yarn and gauge on a separate piece of paper.

MATERIALS

+ FINGERING WEIGHT
(#1 Super Fine) yarn in 100% cotton.
SHOWN HERE Dale of Norway Stork (100% cotton; 195 yards [178 meters]/50 grams): #3 yellow on size U.S. 2 (2.75 mm) needles or size needed to obtain gauge.

+ WORSTED WEIGHT
(#4 Medium) yarn in 100% wool.
SHOWN HERE Cascade 220 Wool (100% wool; 220 yards [201 meters]/100 grams): #8229 green on U.S. size 7 (4.5 mm) needles or size needed to obtain gauge.

+ HEAVY WORSTED WEIGHT
(#4 Medium) yarn in 100% cotton.
SHOWN HERE Filatura di Crosa Porto Cervo Print (100% cotton; 88 yards [80 meters]/50 grams):

#501 multicolored on U.S. size 8 (5 mm) needles or size needed to obtain gauge.

+ CHUNKY WEIGHT
(#5 Bulky) yarn in 100% cotton. **SHOWN HERE** Crystal Palace Cotton Chenille (100% cotton; 98 yards [90 meters/ 50 grams): #1240 lime on U.S. size 6 to 8 (4 to 5 mm) or size needed to obtain gauge.

+ Two double-pointed needles (or one circular needle) in same size needed to get gauge for working hanging loop.

+ Tapestry needle.

+ Pins for blocking.

GAUGE

32 sts and 64 rows (20 stitches and 40 rows, 16 stitches and 32 rows, 14 stitches and 28 rows) = 4" (10 cm) in garter stitch.

Get ready! This project is another square knit on the diagonal, but this one uses two slanting increases and two slanting decreases, plus one double decrease. Add to that the need to keep track of sections of garter stitch and stockinette stitch in the same row and a new skill—the "I-cord" hanging loop—and this project might be a challenge. On the other hand, the inherent regularity in the patterns makes it easy to memorize.

This time, there is a right and a wrong side to the square. It begins at one corner and is shaped by increasing 2 stitches every other row to the desired width, then decreasing 2 stitches every other row to the other corner. The beginning and ending border stitches of each row are knitted in garter stitch (knit every row) to keep the edges from rolling. An inner border of stockinette stitch shows off the shaping. The center is worked in garter stitch so that the piece will form a square shape. If the square were knitted all in stockinette stitch (which has a more elongated row gauge than garter stitch), it would be longer than it is wide, and would form an elongated diamond, not a square.

Slipping the first stitch of each row produces a lovely chain-stitch edge finish, as with the beveled edges that finish off a mirror. In this square, the slipped edges provide the finishing touch.

Four sample squares are shown. The medium green one is worked in the same medium worsted-weight yarn that has been used for the previous projects. The others are worked in different gauges, each in a cotton yarn suitable for washing yourself, a baby, or some dishes. These cotton yarns are not as easy to work with as wool (or some synthetics). They have no "give" or "stretch" or resilience, so irregularities in your tension will be more evident. Your hands will need to get the feel of the yarn and make adjustments to accommodate the difference. You may need to pull less snugly or wrap the yarn with a bigger movement. This is part of becoming an experienced knitter, so let yourself feel the way the yarn wants to be handled.

The yellow sample is knitted in fingering-weight cotton at a gauge of 8 stitches per inch (2.5 cm). This weight of yarn is often used for socks, baby items, and lace. The variegated sample is knitted in a different worsted-weight cotton but it is worked at the gauge usually called "heavy worsted" or "Aran" weight, which is 4 stitches per inch (2.5 cm). The lime green sample is knitted in cotton chenille at a gauge of $3\frac{1}{2}$ stitches per inch (2.5 cm). The pattern is written for these different gauges so that each square has the same finished dimensions. In published patterns, multiple sizes or gauges are indicated by numbers in parentheses. This is partly responsible for why written patterns look so complex to the neophyte.

Note that the top and bottom halves of the square are not identical in appearance. This is because the increases and decreases are not mirror images of each other. The only way to make some knit designs look the same at both ends is to knit both halves out from the center with a provisional cast-on or to make two bottom-up halves and graft them together. Both of these techniques (provisional cast-on and grafting) are very useful, but not covered in this workbook.

Be aware that cotton chenille yarn is very different and, I would say, difficult to work with because it does not stretch or slide past itself. You have to form the stitches without putting any tension on the yarn and you may need to use a very different needle size than you would with wool of a similar thickness. Work this square first in wool or cotton, then move to chenille when you're comfortable with the instructions.

Special Stitches

SL 1 WYF Slip 1 stitch with yarn in front.

 TRANSLATION Slip 1 stitch from the left needle to the right needle, without working it, as if you were going to purl the stitch (see page 73).

PROJECT INSTRUCTIONS

NOTE In this pattern, the odd-numbered rows are wrong-side rows.

CO 6 (4, 4, 4) sts. **TRANSLATION** Cast on the appropriate number of stitches for the yarn you are using. No cast-on method is specified, so use the method of your choice.

 WHY? The cast-on includes the border stitches from each side.

ROW 1 (WS) K across.

ROW 2 (RS) Sl 1 wyf, k2 (1, 1, 1), M1, k3 (2, 2, 2)—7 (5, 5, 5) sts.

 WHY? This row has one increase, setting up an odd number of stitches so that the garter-stitch center will be symmetrical around a single stitch.

 TIP The "make-one" (M1; see page 78) increase is awkward in this row because it's hard to see the strand between the stitches and because there is so little fabric to hold on to. Subsequent rows will be much easier.

+ Add a row marker to help keep track of right- and wrong-side rows.

ROW 3 Sl 1 wyf, k2 (1, 1, 1), p1, k3 (2, 2, 2).

ROW 4 Sl 1 wyf, k2 (1, 1, 1), M1, k1, M1R, k3 (2, 2, 2)—9 (7, 7, 7) sts.

 WHY? This row has two types of make-one increases, one on each side of the center stitch. The two increases are not identical. Their visual differences are subtle but contribute to the overall symmetry.

ROW 5 Sl 1 wyf, k2 (1, 1, 1), p3, k3 (2, 2, 2).

ROW 6 Sl 1 wyf, k2 (1, 1, 1), M1, k3, M1R, k3 (2, 2, 2)—11 (9, 9, 9) sts.

 READ YOUR KNITTING It's time to think about how this pattern can be memorized. The border stitches are knitted on every row. But the first border stitch of the row is always slipped, so you are actually knitting one fewer stitch in the first border. The increases, worked just inside the border, are worked in stockinette stitch. Therefore, the inner border stitches are knitted on right-side (even-numbered) rows and purled on wrong-side rows.

ROW 7 Work for your yarn as follows:
Fingering weight: Sl 1 wyf, k2, p5, k3.
Worsted and heavy worsted weight: Sl 1 wyf, k1, p5, k2.
Chunky weight: (beg garter-st center section) Sl 1 wyf, k1, p2, k1, p2, k2.

 WHY? The different gauges will eventually have different numbers of stitches in their borders. The outer borders already contain 3 (2, 2, 2) stitches at each side. The inner borders will eventually contain 4 (3, 3, 2) stockinette stitches at each side. Once there are enough stitches increased to form the inner and outer borders (7 (5, 5, 4) border stitches at each side, respectively), the remaining

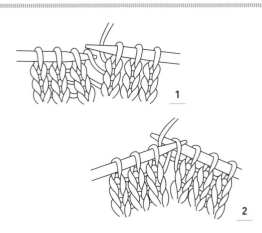

M1 LEFT SLANT (M1 OR M1L) With the left needle tip, lift the strand between the needles (between the last knitted stitch on the right needle and the first stitch on the left needle) from front to back **(FIGURE 1)**, then knit the lifted loop through the back **(FIGURE 2)**—1 stitch increased; increase slants to the left.

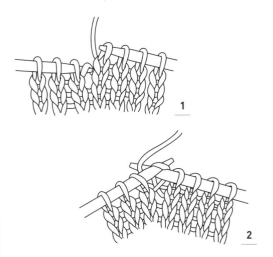

M1 RIGHT SLANT (M1R) With the left needle tip, lift the strand between the needles from back to front **(FIGURE 1)**, then knit the lifted loop through the front **(FIGURE 2)**—1 stitch increased; increase slants to the right.

center stitches are worked in garter stitch. After completing Row 7, only the chunky-weight sample has enough stitches to begin working garter stitch on the center stitch. For the other yarn weights, there will not be enough stitches to begin working the center garter-stitch section until Row 9 for both the worsted and heavy worsted weights (when there are 11 stitches) and Row 11 for fingering weight (when there are 15 stitches).

ROW 8 Sl 1 wyf, k2 (1, 1, 1), M1, k5, M1R, k3 (2, 2, 2)—13 (11, 11, 11) sts.

ROW 9 Work for your yarn as follows:
Fingering weight: Sl 1 wyf, k2, p7, k3.
Worsted and heavy worsted weight: (beg garter-st center section) Sl 1 wyf, k1, p3, k1, p3, k2.
Chunky weight: Sl 1 wyf, k1, p2, k3, p2, k2.

ROW 10 Sl 1 wyf, k2 (1, 1, 1), M1, k to last 3 (2, 2, 2) sts, M1R, k3 (2, 2, 2)—15 (13, 13, 13) sts.

ROW 11 Work for your yarn as follows:
Fingering weight: (beg garter-st center section) Sl 1 wyf, k2, p4, k1, p4, k3.
Worsted and heavy worsted weight: Sl 1 wyf, k1, p3, k3, p3, k2.
Chunky weight: Sl 1 wyf, k1, p2, k5, p2, k2.

ROW 12 Sl 1 wyf, k2 (1, 1, 1), M1, k to last 3 (2, 2, 2) sts, M1R, k3 (2, 2, 2)—2 sts increased.

ROW 13 Sl 1 wyf, k2 (1, 1, 1), p4 (3, 3, 2), k to last 7 (5, 5, 4) sts, p4 (3, 3, 2), k3 (2, 2, 2).

Rep Rows 12 and 13 until the diagonal side edges measure 7¼" (18.5 cm), ending with a WS row.

? **WHY?** In this case, we want to measure the length of our knitting along the diagonal edges because that is how the width or length of the square is measured. We want to end up with an 8" (20.5 cm) square.

📖 **READ YOUR KNITTING** While working these rows, you should become accustomed to the regularity of the pattern and be able to work it from memory. All of the increases are made on right-side rows and, except for the first slipped stitch, all of the other right-side row stitches are knitted. On wrong-side rows, the first stitch is slipped, the outer border and center stitches are knitted, and the inner border stitches are purled. You do need to keep track of the number of border stitches. Markers aren't practical to use, because they will get in the way of the increases and later decreases—they would have to be moved every other row.

💡 **TIP** How can you tell the right from the wrong side? Use the stockinette-stitch inner borders as a guide—they appear as knit stitches on right-side rows and as purl stitches on wrong-side rows.

Work 4 (2, 2, 2) rows even.

🔄 **TRANSLATION** To "work even" means to keep the pattern as established without performing any increases or decreases. In this pattern, you will continue to slip the first stitch of every row, work the outer borders in garter stitch, the inner borders in stockinette stitch, and the center in garter stitch, but you will not work any increases.

? **WHY?** Working a few rows even will help the corners lie flat.

NEXT ROW (RS; DEC ROW) Sl 1 wyf, k2 (1, 1, 1), ssk, k to last 5 (4, 4, 4) sts, k2tog, k3 (2, 2, 2)—2 sts decreased.

🔄 **TRANSLATION** This is the first decrease row. The slipped stitch and first garter-stitch outer border are maintained, followed by a left-leaning ssk (see page 81) decrease. The second decrease, a right-leaning k2tog decrease, is made just before the second garter-stitch outer border.

? **WHY?** Because this is a right-side row, both the stockinette inner border and the garter center section are worked as knit stitches. This is why the instruction can be written to just knit across to where the second decrease needs to be made.

NEXT ROW (WS) Rep Row 13.

Rep the last 2 rows until 15 (11, 11, 9) sts rem, ending with a WS row.

NEXT ROW Rep dec row 1 more time—13 (9, 9, 7) sts rem.

NEXT ROW (WS) Sl 1 wyf, k2 (1, 1, 1), p to last 3 (2, 2, 2) sts, k3 (2, 2, 2).

📖 **READ YOUR KNITTING** Notice that all of the garter-stitch center stitches have been consumed by decreases so that no more knit stitches are worked in the center of wrong-side rows.

Rep the last 2 rows 2 (1, 1, 0) more time(s)—9 (7, 7, 7) sts rem.

🔄 **TRANSLATION** There is a "no repeat" phrase in these instructions—indicated by "0 times" an action is to be repeated. This is only necessary when a pattern is written for multiple gauges or sizes and a particular instruction does not apply to one (or more) of the sizes. In this case, the fingering-weight version needs two more repeats of the decrease row, the worsted-weight and heavy worsted-weight versions need one more repeat of the decrease row, and the chunky-weight version needs no additional repeats of the decrease row to achieve the desired number of stitches. It especially helpful to highlight the numbers that apply to your size on a photocopy of the pattern.

NEXT ROW (RS) Sl 1 wyf, k2 (1, 1, 1), sl 2 tog kwise, k1, p2sso (one double decrease made), k3 (2, 2, 2)—7 (5, 5, 5) sts rem.

 TRANSLATION The double decrease eliminates 2 stitches at once (see page 81). This decrease slants to the left.

NEXT ROW Sl 1 wyf, k2 (1, 1, 1), p1, k3 (2, 2, 2).

NEXT ROW Sl 1 wyf, k across.

NEXT ROW For fingering-weight yarn only: Sl 1 wyf, ssk, k1, k2tog, k1—5 sts rem. For all other weights of yarn: Sl 1 wyf, ssk, k2—4 sts rem.

OPTIONAL **To omit hanging loop**

BO knitwise. Weave in ends.
Block to measurements if desired.

OPTIONAL **Hanging loop**

If using straight needles, slip stitches to double-pointed needle. Work 5 (4, 4, 4) st I-cord for 3" (7.5 cm) or desired length.

 TIP See page 81 for I-cord instructions. I-cord creates a very small-diameter tube. Notice as you work that the right side of the piece is always facing you and as a consequence, stockinette-stitch fabric (not garter stitch) is produced as you knit every row. Give a strong lengthwise tug on the I-cord every few rows to tighten up the yarn and even out the stitches.

BO. Break yarn, leaving a 6" (15 cm) tail. Thread tail on a tapestry needle and use it to sew hanging loop to WS of top of square.

 WHY? The usual way to finish off I-cord is to leave the stitches on the needle, break the yarn, thread it onto a tapestry needle, and thread the yarn tail through the stitches on the knitting needle, pulling out the knitting needle as you go. Then the yarn tail is pulled tight to pull the stitches together, and the yarn tail is fastened off. For our square, however, we want a straight bind-off that makes a neater edge to sew to the back of the square.

Weave in ends. Block to measurements, if desired.

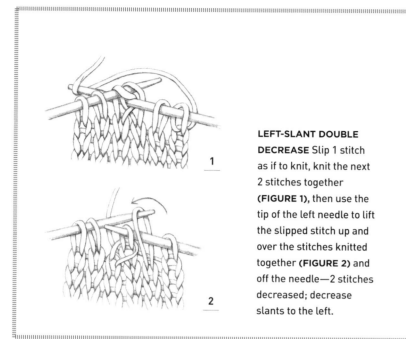

LEFT-SLANT DOUBLE DECREASE Slip 1 stitch as if to knit, knit the next 2 stitches together **(FIGURE 1)**, then use the tip of the left needle to lift the slipped stitch up and over the stitches knitted together **(FIGURE 2)** and off the needle—2 stitches decreased; decrease slants to the left.

I-CORD Using two double-pointed needles, cast on the desired number of stitches (usually between 3 and 5 stitches) if they are not already on the needle. Knit across the stitches with right side facing, then *without turning the needle, slide the stitches to the other tip of the needle, pull the yarn around the back, and knit the stitches as usual (again from the right side). Repeat from * for the desired length.

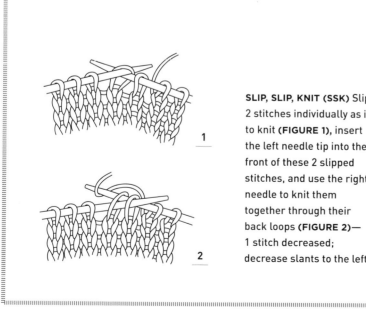

SLIP, SLIP, KNIT (SSK) Slip 2 stitches individually as if to knit **(FIGURE 1)**, insert the left needle tip into the front of these 2 slipped stitches, and use the right needle to knit them together through their back loops **(FIGURE 2)**— 1 stitch decreased; decrease slants to the left.

Extra Credit
Heart-Shaped Leaf

FINISHED SIZE

About 8" (20.5 cm) wide and 9½" (24 cm) long, excluding stem.

MATERIALS

+ Worsted-weight yarn (#4 Medium).
SHOWN HERE Cascade 220 Wool (100% wool; 220 yards [201 meters]/100 grams): #8229 green.

+ Size U.S. 7 (4.5 mm) straight and 2 double-pointed needles or size needed to obtain gauge.

+ Stitch holder.

+ Tapestry needle.

+ Pins for blocking.

GAUGE

20 stitches and 28 rows = 4" (10 cm); 5 stitches and 7 rows = 1" (2.5 cm) in stockinette stitch, after blocking.

NOTES

+ In the garter-stitch border, "inc 1" means "k1f&b," which uses 1 stitch and counts as 2 stitches after the increase has been completed; "k2tog" and "ssk" each use 2 stitches and result in 1 stitch after the decrease has been completed.

+ Even-numbered rows are wrong-side rows.

+ Increases are to be worked as k1f&b.

Practice following complex row-by-row instructions, similar to those used to shape necklines and sleeve caps in garments.

This piece is a complex shape formed using multiple techniques. From a single cast-on stitch, the shape grows with symmetric increases, all made by knitting into the front and back of a single stitch (see page 85), making 2 stitches from 1. The increases are made at different rates, first every other row, then every row, then every other row again. This means that some increases are worked on right-side rows and some are worked on wrong-side rows.

The instructions that follow are written out row by row. A chart is also provided (omitting the I-cord stem), but first try to follow the shaping instructions from the words. The words will give you a taste of complex shaping instructions in sweater patterns, such as for sleeve caps.

The leaf piece introduces a common shaping technique, dividing the stitches and working parts separately. This technique is often used in sweater construction for the separate shoulder areas between the neck opening and each armhole edge, where each side is worked separately at

the same time, or where the stitches for one side are placed on a stitch holder to be worked later. The last few right-side rows of the leaf omit the purled reverse-stockinette stitches so that the top border is garter stitch. As a finishing touch, a short stem is worked in I-cord (see page 81).

Often, patterns say to increase (abbreviated "inc") without specifying which form of increase to use, in which case you can choose a method. However, when patterns say to "inc 1 in" a stitch, it means to use an increase worked into an existing stitch. Remember that the M1 and yarnover increases create a stitch between 2 existing stitches; other stitches are not involved in these increases. In this project, I used the bar increase, so named because it results in a small visible horizontal bar. The bar increase is abbreviated k1f&b because it involves knitting into the front and back "loop" of the same stitch, as described on page 85. Sometimes instructions in this project say "inc 1" and sometimes they say "inc in" a specific stitch, but all increases are to be performed as bar increases.

PROJECT INSTRUCTIONS

CO 1 st.

ROW 1 (RS) Inc 1.

ROW 2 (WS) K2.

ROW 3 Inc 1 in each st.

ROW 4 K4.

ROW 5 Inc 1, k2, inc 1.

ROW 6 K6.

ROW 7 Inc 1, k4, inc 1.

ROW 8 Inc 1, k2, p2, k2, inc 1.

ROW 9 Inc 1, [k2, p1] 2 times, k2, inc 1.

ROW 10 Inc 1, k4, p2, k4, inc 1—14 sts.

Keeping the first 4 and last 4 sts of every row in garter st, center 2 sts in St st, and all other sts in reverse St st, continue shaping as foll: Inc in the first and last st of every row 5 times, then every other row 9 times, ending with RS Row 33—42 sts.

💡 TIP This is about as complex as instructions can get, with multiple areas of shaping and stitch patterns going on at once. You will need to develop your own way to cope with this—write out each

row separately, chart the stitches (I've done this for you on page 87), make notes on your pattern, or whatever works for you.

📖 **READ YOUR KNITTING** To tell when you are done shaping without counting all of the rows individually, note that the shaping is symmetrical and that the goal at the end of shaping is 42 stitches. This means that each half will end up with 21 stitches. It is easier to count stitches than rows. When you get close to 21 stitches on each side, add a marker to set off a convenient number of stitches (such as 15) that you won't have to count again, then just count the number of stitches needed to get to 21. On the last wrong-side row, count the number of stitches in the entire piece to confirm that there are 42 stitches, just in case you missed an increase or miscounted.

ROWS 34–56 Keeping in pattern as established, work 23 rows even, beg and ending with a WS row.

💡 TIP Add a row marker to the first of the 23 rows to help you keep track of where these 23 rows begin.

ROW 57 (RS; DEC ROW) Keeping in pattern as established, ssk, work to last 2 sts, k2tog—2 sts decreased.

ROWS 58–63 *Work 1 WS row even, then work dec row; rep from * 2 more times—34 sts rem.

📖 **READ YOUR KNITTING** Again, it will be easier to count the stitches than the rows.

💡 TIP To maintain the 4-stitch garter border as established, begin working the knit stitches 5 stitches from the end of a decrease row (the k2tog will reduce the last 2 stitches into 1 stitch— see Notes).

ROW 64 (WS; DIVIDING ROW) K14, ssk, p2, place these 17 sts onto a holder, k2tog, k14—15 sts rem.

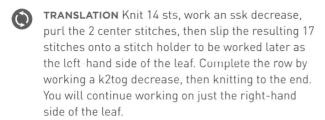

TRANSLATION Knit 14 sts, work an ssk decrease, purl the 2 center stitches, then slip the resulting 17 stitches onto a stitch holder to be worked later as the left-hand side of the leaf. Complete the row by working a k2tog decrease, then knitting to the end. You will continue working on just the right-hand side of the leaf.

TIP Work the decreases as stated. Because this is a wrong-side row, the decreases will slant away from the center p2 column as is needed for the top parts of the leaf.

Right-hand side leaf top

ROW 65 (RS) Ssk, k3, p7, k1, k2tog.

ROWS 66 AND 68 K across.

ROW 67 [Ssk] 2 times, k5, [k2tog] 2 times.

ROW 69 [Ssk] 2 times, k1, [k2tog] 2 times.

ROW 70 K5.

BO knitwise.

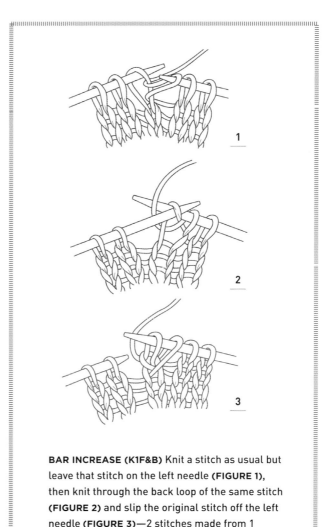

BAR INCREASE (K1F&B) Knit a stitch as usual but leave that stitch on the left needle **(FIGURE 1)**, then knit through the back loop of the same stitch **(FIGURE 2)** and slip the original stitch off the left needle **(FIGURE 3)**—2 stitches made from 1 stitch; 1 stitch increased.

Left-hand side leaf top

Return stitches from holder to needles. With RS facing, attach yarn at center edge.

ROW 65 (RS) K2, place these 2 sts on holder for I-cord stem, ssk, k1, p7, k3, k2tog—13 sts rem.

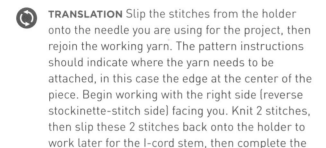 **TRANSLATION** Slip the stitches from the holder onto the needle you are using for the project, then rejoin the working yarn. The pattern instructions should indicate where the yarn needs to be attached, in this case the edge at the center of the piece. Begin working with the right side (reverse stockinette-stitch side) facing you. Knit 2 stitches, then slip these 2 stitches back onto the holder to work later for the I-cord stem, then complete the row as indicated, with the slanted decreases, knits, and purls.

TIP There are two ways to attach the yarn. You can thread the yarn through the first stitch to be worked and tie a knot (tie it loosely so you can untie it before weaving in the end later), or (as I prefer) just start knitting with the yarn without knotting it. Either way, the tension may be loose on the first few stitches—you'll fix this when you weave in the ends.

ROWS 66 AND 68 (WS) K across.

ROW 67 [Ssk] 2 times, k5, [k2tog] 2 times.

ROW 69 [Ssk] 2 times, k1, [k2tog] 2 times.

ROW 70 K5.

BO all sts knitwise.

Stem

Place 2 held stem sts on double-pointed needle. With RS facing, reattach yarn at right-hand edge. K1f&b in each st—4 sts. Work 4-st I-cord for 1½" (3.8 cm) or to desired length. Break yarn, leaving a 6" (15 cm) tail. Thread tail on a tapestry needle, draw it through all sts on needle, draw up, and fasten off.

Weave in ends. Block to shape.

TIP To weave in the I-cord tail, run it down through the center of the I-cord. Before weaving in the other ends, unfasten any knots you made when attaching the yarn, then even up the tension if necessary by pulling on the neighboring stitches with a crochet hook or the tip of the tapestry needle. While blocking, curve the sides by patting and pinning them to the desired shape. Straighten the center vein by laying a ruler alongside it as you pull and pat it into shape.

HEART-SHAPED LEAF

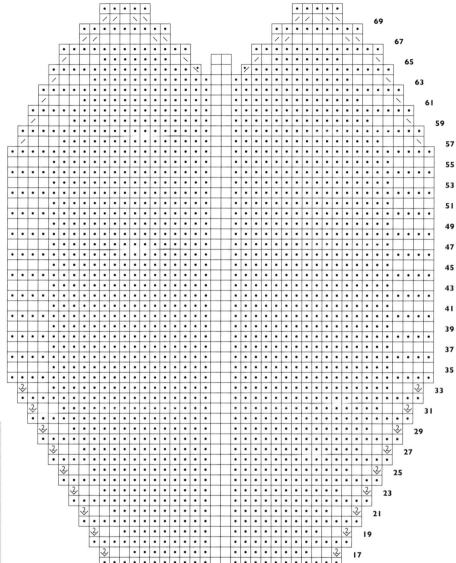

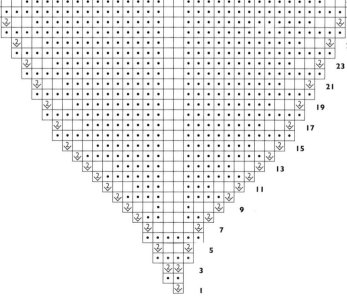

69
67
65
63
61
59
57
55
53
51
49
47
45
43
41
39
37
35
33
31
29
27
25
23
21
19
17
15
13
11
9
7
5
3
1

CHART KEY

☐	k on RS; p on WS
•	p on RS; k on WS
╱	k2tog
╲	ssk
✗	p2tog on RS; k2tog on WS
╲	ssp on RS; ssk on WS
⅋	k1 f&b

EXPANDED BASIC CABLE SQUARE, PAGE 98

04

YOU'RE OUT OF ORDER!
CABLES AND CROSSED STITCHES

Cables are intimidating to many new knitters. There are probably three reasons for this. First, cables are impressively dimensional and sumptuous and therefore they must be difficult, right? How could you possibly get the fabric to twist like that simply by knitting and purling? Is yoga involved? The second reason is that cable needles have a mysterious look to them. They are shaped like crooks or notched bars that may remind you of dental implements used for, well, let's not even think about what. Third, the written descriptions for making cables, the names given to the procedures, and the charts, are much more confusing than the actual knitting required.

In fact, cables are easy! If you can knit and slip stitches (move them from one needle to another without working them or twisting them), you can make cables. It's the easiest way to add that extra "I'm a Real Knitter Now and Not a Beginner" touch to your work—much easier than lace or working with multiple colors.

The basic maneuver required to form a cable is to slip some stitches off of the left needle onto a spare implement and hold them aside while you work the next stitches on the left needle as usual with your right needle. Then, treat the spare implement as the left needle and knit the stitches off of that implement, then continue across the row as usual. By doing this you have worked a group of stitches out of their usual order. That's it. That's the entire secret of cables.

But how, you may be thinking, do you create all of the complicated cables in Aran sweaters, going every which way, made up of different stitches, and forming diamonds and ladders and braids? The answer is in the number of stitches used in the cables and how and how often the maneuver is performed. Even the most ornate cable patterns can be broken down into individual maneuvers that can be mixed and expanded.

THE NUMBER OF STITCHES. A small, simple cable might be formed over 4 stitches, 2 that are set aside while 2 other stitches are worked. Wider cables are formed by setting aside more stitches.

HOW OFTEN THE CABLE IS TWISTED. The more rows in between the cable twists, the longer and looser the cable will appear.

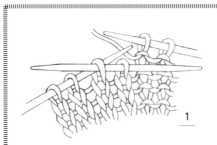

1

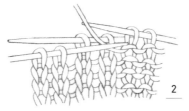

2

3

TWISTING CABLES Slip the designated number of stitches (2 shown) onto a cable needle, hold the cable needle in front of the work for a left-leaning twist **(FIGURE 1)** or in back of the work for a right-leaning twist **(FIGURE 2)**, knit the specified number of stitches from the left needle (usually the same number of stitches that were placed on the cable needle), then work the stitches from the cable needle in the order in which they were placed on the needle **(FIGURE 3)**.

WHERE THE SLIPPED STITCHES ARE HELD. Whether the slipped stitches are held to the front or to the back of the work as the adjacent stitches are worked will determine if the cable twists to the right (if held in back) or to the left (if held in front) as you face it. If the slipped stitches are always held on the same side (front or back), the basic ropy look is produced.

THE TYPE OF STITCHES WORKED. Most basic cables are worked in stockinette stitch. You can create interesting effects if you work some of the stitches in reverse stockinette stitch, seed stitch, or ribbing.

THE SURROUNDING STITCHES. Most basic stockinette-stitch cables are bounded by one or more purl stitches. But it's perfectly acceptable to use other background stitches or to position cables right next to each other without surrounding stitches in between.

The projects in this section will take you from a single basic cable repeated multiple times through cables that vary in size and stitch pattern, ending with several variations in a single square. This is where cable knitting does become difficult. But it's not the knitting itself that is difficult. It's keeping track of the variation.

What about the "spare implement" I mentioned? The key is that it needs to have a point at each end—one end for slipping the stitches onto and the other end for knitting the stitches off of. You can use a cable needle of any shape as long as its diameter is smaller than the knitting needles you're using (otherwise the stitches may have to stretch to fit on the cable needle). If you don't have a "true" cable needle, you can substitute a spare double-pointed needle, crochet hook (slip the stitches with the hook end and knit them off of the straight end), chopstick, pencil. . . .You get the idea. Although true cable needles are convenient, you don't have to rush out to buy one in order to knit the squares in this section.

Blocking, as always, will improve the look of your knitting, but be careful when blocking cables, especially when using a steam iron. Never press down on a cable, unless your intention is to flatten it.

Tinking Cables: Anticipating and Fixing Mistakes

A common mistake in cabling is to hold the slipped stitches on the wrong side of the work so that the cable twists in the wrong direction. It is possible to fix this mistake without ripping out entire rows, but doing so requires a sure mastery of reading your knitting and is best learned when you have more experience. If you want to fix such a mistake while knitting one of the squares in this section, tink (see page 45) back to the where the cable was twisted, use the cable needle to un-knit the first stitches of the cable (the ones that were knitted last and that were originally held by the cable needle), tink the remaining cable stitches onto the left needle, then rework the cable, this time holding the cable needle to the correct side of the work.

Basic Cable Square

FINISHED SIZE

About 8" (20.5 cm) square.

MATERIALS

+ Worsted-weight yarn
(#4 Medium).

SHOWN HERE Cascade 220 Wool
(100% wool; 220 yards
[201 meters]/100 grams):
#8420 purple.

+ Size U.S. 7 (4.5 mm)
needles or size needed
to obtain gauge.

+ Cable needle (cn).

+ Tapestry needle.

+ Pins for blocking.

GAUGE

20 stitches and 28 rows =
4" (10 cm); 5 stitches and
7 rows = 1" (2.5 cm) in
stockinette stitch, after
blocking.

Learn to use a cable needle to twist cables—a simple matter of reversing the order of a group of stitches.

This project introduces a simple pattern of three 6-stitch wide stockinette cables on a reverse-stockinette background. The cables are all twisted every 8 rows. By the time you finish this square, you'll be comfortable with twisting cables and you'll be familiar with how instructions and charts for cables are presented. Rest easy—the instructions and charts are more confusing than the actual knitting. The instructions are presented in several forms to make you aware of the different ways cable patterns can be presented. Sometimes cable stitches are given names based on where the slipped stitches are held (front or back) or the direction that the cable twists (left or right). Some cables simply have descriptive names (for example, antler, stag horn, horseshoe, and honeycomb).

This square involves increasing stitches at the base of each cable and decreasing stitches at the top of each cable. These increases and decreases are not required for cables per se, but they help counteract the tendency that cables have to significantly pull in the knitting sideways. This "pull in" means that more stitches are needed to maintain an 8" (20.5 cm) width. If the initial cast on included the extra stitches for each cable, the border would have more stitches than needed for an 8" (20.5 cm) width and the top and bottom edges would flare instead of lying flat.

Special Stitches

3/3RC Sl 3 sts onto cn and hold in back, k3, k3 from cn.

 TRANSLATION For this pattern, the cable maneuver has been named 3/3RC, which stands for "3-over-3 right cross" or "3-over-3 right cable." Because cables do not have universal names, the stitches will be explained in the instructions. "3/3RC" indicates a 6-stitch cable formed with knit stitches, in which the first 3 stitches are slipped onto a cable needle and held in back of the work while the next 3 stitches are worked to produce a cable that that crosses to the right as you face it.

 TIP Unless otherwise specified, always slip stitches onto the cable needle "as if to purl." In this case, hold the yarn to the back as you insert the cable needle from the back to the front into the stitches on the left needle (as if you were going to purl them) one at a time without working them. The slipped stitches will be on the cable needle in their original orientation. Next, drop the cable needle to the back of your work so that it rests behind the knitting needles and behind the working yarn. Knit the next 3 stitches on the left knitting needle, pulling the yarn tight when knitting the first stitch to close the gap between the last stitch knitted and the current stitch. Push the rest of the stitches on the left needle away from the tip so they don't inadvertently drop off and let go of the left needle. Pick up the cable needle in your left hand (be sure that the cable needle isn't twisted), push the 3 slipped stitches to the right tip of the cable needle, then knit these 3 stitches as usual. The stitches will be tight because they have to stretch to reach across the last 3 knitted stitches. Work these stitches close to the tapered tip of the cable needle.

PROJECT INSTRUCTIONS

CO 40 sts.

ROW 1 *K1, p1; rep from * across.

ROW 2 *P1, k1; rep from * across.

ROWS 3–5 Rep Rows 1 and 2 once, then rep Row 1 once more.

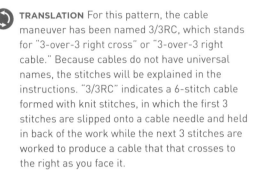 **WHY?** The previous squares in this workbook had 4 rows in the seed-stitch borders. This square requires 5 rows to allow for a wrong-side set-up row in which increases are made to accommodate the "pull in" of the cables. These increases are easiest and least visible if they are knitted, which, in this pattern, happens on wrong-side rows. For this square, I initially worked a 3-row seed-stitch border, but it looked too narrow on the completed piece. As the knitter working from a published pattern, you don't need to worry about things like this, but it may help you understand why a designer has included something that doesn't make immediate sense. There may be a behind-the-scenes reason for it.

ROW 6 (WS; SET-UP ROW) P1, k1, p1, k6, M1, *p6, [M1, k1] 2 times; rep from * once more, p6, M1, k7, p1, k1—46 sts.

TRANSLATION A "set-up row" is a row used to set up the stitches for a pattern to come. The instructions may include adding or removing stitches, adding markers, or working stitches in a specific way to prepare them for the upcoming pattern. A set-up row is usually worked only once at the beginning of a pattern. This set-up row involves increases (M1; see page 78) and there should be 46 stitches when the row has been completed.

WHY? The set-up row accomplishes two things. It increases the number of stitches by 6 to 46 stitches. Why? Cable stitches pull in horizontally, so we will need more than 40 stitches to maintain the desired 8" (20.5 cm) width. Why increase 6 stitches? According to Barbara Walker's *Third Treasury of Knitting Patterns,* a rule of thumb is to increase 1 or 2 stitches for each cable. Based on a preliminary swatch that I knitted, I determined that 6 was the appropriate number of stitches to increase. Secondly, the set-up row establishes the knit and purl sequence that will be used for the cable pattern. Notice that because it is a wrong-side row, the knits and purls are reversed.

 TIP After working the set-up row, check your stitches carefully to make sure that there are the correct number of stitches and that the sequence of knits and purls matches the instructions.

Cable pattern (8-row rep)

ROW 7 (RS) K1, p1, k1, p7, k6, [p4, k6] 2 times, end p8, k1, p1.

ROWS 8, 10, 12, AND 14 P1, k1, p1, k7 [p6, k4] 2 times, end p6, k8, p1, k1.

ROW 9 K1, p1, k1, p7, *3/3RC, p4; rep from * 2 more times, end p4, k1, p1.

TIP When you're ready to work the 3/3RC cable, read the instructions in Special Stitches carefully.

ROWS 11 AND 13 Rep Row 7.

ROWS 15–51 Rep Rows 7–14 four more times, then work Rows 7–11 once more.

ROW 52 (DEC ROW) P1, k1, p1, k5, k2tog, p6, [k2tog] 2 times, p6, [k2tog] 2 times, p6, k2tog, k6, p1, k1—40 sts rem.

WHY? This decrease row (abbreviated "dec") eliminates the 6 extra stitches that were added in the set-up row. The result is that the top border will have the same number of stitches as the bottom border.

ROWS 53–57 Work seed st across all sts as established by seed st borders.

BO in patt. Weave in ends. Block to measurements.

04

You're out of order!
CABLES AND
CROSSED STITCHES

Working from a Chart

Long, involved row-by-row instruction can be like driving through fog. It's difficult to see very far down the road, and it can be hard to tell if you're even on the right road, especially if you don't know what your work is supposed to look like along the way. A chart can help you see the "big picture" by showing how the stitches in one row relate to the stitches in adjacent rows, thereby giving you a sense of where you're going.

From the chart, right, you can see that that there is a 3-stitch seed-stitch border, three columns of 6-stitch stockinette-stitch cables that are twisted every 8 rows, 7 reverse stockinette stitches between the border and the cables, and 4 reverse stockinette stitches between the cables. You can use markers to separate the different stitch patterns or read your knitting after the set-up row to know how to work each row.

But what are those gray cells that are designated as "no stitch"? What kind of Zen thing is this, the stitch that is no stitch? The "no stitch" symbol is used as a place holder for a stitch that will be introduced in a subsequent row, or a stitch that has been eliminated in a previous row. After the increases are worked in Row 6, the chart has to show 46 stitches, not the 40 that were worked for the border. These extra 6 stitches could be added all together at the left edge of the chart on Row 6, but doing so would mean that the cells in Row 6 would not align properly with the cells in Rows 1–5, and the chart would be less helpful as a visual representation of the finished swatch. When you come to a no-stitch symbol, simply understand that it is there only to maintain vertical alignment of the charted symbols, not to instruct you to do anything special. Just skip over

it (because it doesn't represent anything on your needles) and move onto the next stitch.

READ YOUR KNITTING

As long as you know whether you're on a right-side or a wrong-side row, the sequence of stitches (except for the cable maneuvers) should be pretty easy to follow now. After Row 6, right-side rows involve working 3 seed stitches, 7 purl stitches, 6 knit stitches, 4 purl stitches, 6 knit stitches, etc. Simply look at the previous row of knitting to know when to change from seed stitch to reverse stockinette to stockinette, and so on.

READ YOUR KNITTING

The chart shows that the cable maneuvers are repeated every 8 rows, beginning with Row 9, and that there are a total of 6 cable-cross rows. If you can read your knitting and count the rows between cables, you'll know when to cross the cables without

looking at the chart or instructions for Rows 9 to 49. Simply follow the pattern "as established." Be aware that it can be hard to count the number of rows between cables, especially if you have trouble identifying the cable-twist rows. From the written instructions, you can only be sure that the twists happen somewhere between Rows 7 and 14. From the chart, you can see that they occur on Rows 9, 17, 25, 33, 41, and 49, but what if you lose count along the way?

TIP Place a row marker near the beginning of a cable-twist row and designate that row as the first row in the cable sequence. Then you only need to count from 1 to 8 before it's time for another twist row. Move the row marker up each time you work a cable-twist row. Once you've completed all 6 cable-twist rows, refer to the instructions or chart to know what to do next.

If it helps you keep track, note how you count the rows on a photocopy of the pattern.

When working a cable project from written instructions alone, try charting the pattern for yourself. Even charting just the cable-twist row (Row 7) on ordinary graph paper will help you see the "big picture" of the pattern.

BASIC CABLE

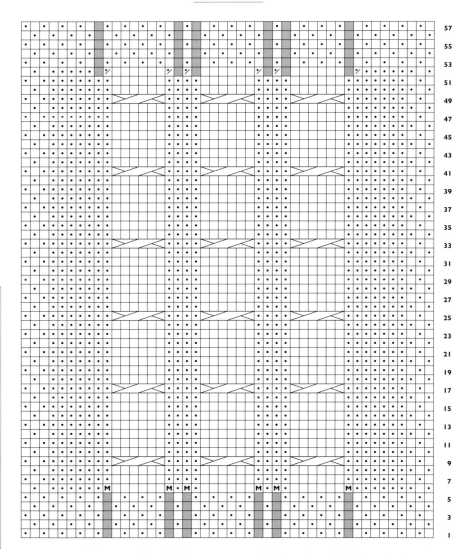

CHART KEY

☐ k on RS; p on WS

• p on RS; k on WS

⟋ p2tog on RS; k2tog on WS

M M1

▨ no stitch

⟋⟍ 3/3RC: sl 3 sts onto cn and hold in back, k3, k3 from cn

04

You're out of order!
CABLES AND
CROSSED STITCHES

Expanded Basic Cable Square

FINISHED SIZE

About 8" (20.5 cm) square.

MATERIALS

+ Worsted-weight yarn
(#4 Medium).

SHOWN HERE Cascade 220
Wool (100% wool; 220 yards
[201 meters]/100 grams):
#8420 purple.

+ Size U.S. 7 (4.5 mm)
needles or size needed
to obtain gauge.

+ Cable needle (cn).

+ Tapestry needle.

+ Pins for blocking.

GAUGE

20 stitches and 28 rows = 4"
(10 cm); 5 stitches and 7 rows
= 1" (2.5 cm) in stockinette
stitch, after blocking.

Cables will twist to the left or right, depending on whether the cable needle is held in front or back.

This square has a 3/3RC cable on the right-hand side, a 3/3LC cable (the stitches on the cable needle are held in front so they cross to the left) on the left-hand side, and a horseshoe cable (formed by working a 3/3RC right before a 3/3LC without any background stitches between them) in the center.

The instructions are written for an abbreviated chart that shows a single 8-row repeat of the cable pattern. A complete chart is also provided for reference.

PROJECT INSTRUCTIONS

CO 40 sts.

ROWS 1–5 Work in k1, p1 seed st as for Basic Cable Square (see page 92).

ROW 6 (WS: SET-UP ROW) P1, k1, p1, M1, k3, M1, p6, M1, k3, M1, p3, M1P, p4, M1P, p3, M1, k3, M1, p6, M1, k3, M1, k1, p1, k1—50 sts.

? **WHY?** Because the set-up row is a wrong-side row, the knits and purls are reversed. Two of the increases are needed in the stockinette-stitch section, so purlwise increases (M1P; see page 101) are specified for these stitches.

💡 **TIP** After working the set-up row, count the stitches and verify that the knit and purl sequence matches the instructions.

ROWS 7–51 Keeping first 3 and last 3 sts in seed st for border, work Rows 1–8 of the Minimal Expanded Basic Cable chart across 44 stitches 5 times, then rep Rows 1–5 of chart once more.

? **WHY?** The first cable twist occurs on the third row of the 8-row repeated sequence and the last cable twist occurs on the third row from the end of the last 5 rows of the sequence. Why? There must be some stockinette-stitch rows before the first cable is twisted so that there is some fabric to twist. For symmetry, 2 rows are worked before the first cable is twisted and 2 rows are worked after the last cable is twisted.

💡 **TIP** Use stitch markers to separate the borders from the center 44 stitches and to separate the columns of stockinette and reverse stockinette

MINIMAL EXPANDED BASIC CABLE

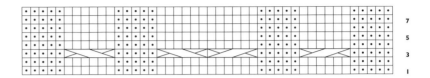

EXPANDED BASIC CABLE

CHART KEY

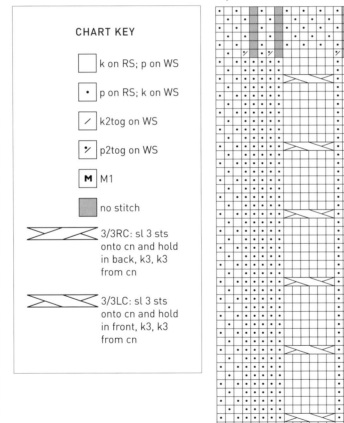

k on RS; p on WS

· p on RS; k on WS

/ k2tog on WS

⟍ p2tog on WS

M M1

no stitch

3/3RC: sl 3 sts onto cn and hold in back, k3, k3 from cn

3/3LC: sl 3 sts onto cn and hold in front, k3, k3 from cn

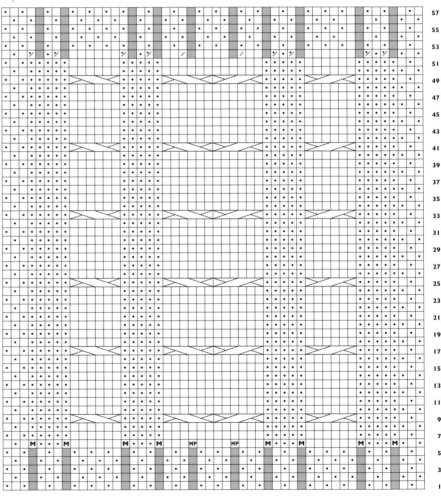

stitch. Also, mark the cable row with a row marker and mentally count this as row 1 of the 8-row repeat. Once the pattern is established, you can count the rows between cables and the completed cables until you finish the sixth cable row. Then refer back to the instructions and chart to determine that 2 more rows are needed after the last cable.

ROW 52 (DEC ROW) P1, k1, p1, k2tog, k1, k2tog, p6, k2tog, k1, k2tog, p2, p2tog, p4, p2tog, p2, k2tog, k1, k2tog, p6, k2tog, k1, k2tog, k1, p1, k1—40 sts rem.

🔄 **TRANSLATION** In this decrease row, the 10 stitches added in the set-up row are decreased while the sequence of knit and purl stitches is maintained.

❓ **WHY?** This row returns the stitch count to the original 40 by decreasing 10 stitches across the row. Two of these decreases occur on the wrong-side (purl) row of a stockinette-stitch section, so the "purl 2 together" (p2tog) decrease is used (see at right).

ROWS 53–57 Work in seed st across all sts as established by seed st borders.

BO in patt. Weave in ends. Block to measurements.

Special Stitches

3/3RC Sl 3 sts onto cn and hold in back, k3, k3 from cn.

🔄 **TRANSLATION** In this case, 3/3RC refers to a stockinette-stitch 6-stitch cable in which 3 stitches on the cable needle are held in the back of the work so that the cable will cross to the right as you face it.

3/3LC Sl 3 sts onto cn and hold in front, k3, k3 from cn.

🔄 **TRANSLATION** In this case, 3/3LC refers to a stockinette-stitch 6-stitch cable in which 3 stitches on the cable needle are held in the front of the work so that the cable will cross to the left as you face it.

💡 **TIP** Unless otherwise specified, always slip the stitches "as if to purl."

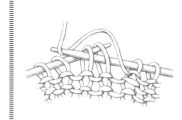

PURL 2 TOGETHER (P2TOG) Purl 2 stitches together as if they were a single stitch—1 stitch decreased; decrease slants to the right.

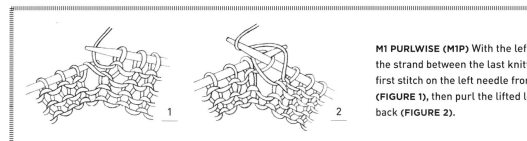

M1 PURLWISE (M1P) With the left needle tip, lift the strand between the last knitted stitch and the first stitch on the left needle from front to back **(FIGURE 1)**, then purl the lifted loop through the back **(FIGURE 2)**.

Multitasking Cable Square

FINISHED SIZE

About 8" (20.5 cm) square.

MATERIALS

+ Worsted-weight yarn
(#4 Medium).

SHOWN HERE Cascade 220 Wool
(100% wool; 220 yards
[201 meters]/100 grams):
#8420 purple.

+ Size U.S. 7 (4.5 mm)
needles or size needed to
obtain gauge.

+ Cable needle (cn).

+ Tapestry needle.

+ Pins for blocking.

GAUGE

20 stitches and 28 rows = 4"
(10 cm); 5 stitches and 7 rows
= 1" (2.5 cm) in stockinette
stitch, after blocking.

In this square, you'll keep track of left- and right-twisting cables of different widths and lengths.

This square introduces crossing 2 stitches without a cable needle, called "right twist" or "left twist," depending on the direction that the stitches cross. Also the cables are different widths and do not all cross on the same row. The two 4-stitch cables cross to the right or left every 4 rows. The center cable is 8 stitches wide, crosses every 10 rows, and is formed from 4 stockinette stitches and 4 seed stitches. The challenge is in managing the constant variation. The cable maneuvers themselves are no harder than the ones in the Basic Cable Square (see page 92), although the right and left twists will feel awkward at first.

Published patterns often provide a separate (minimal) chart for each type of cable, leaving it up to the knitter to put them together horizontally across a row. The written instructions for this square are based on the minimal charts, but a complete chart is also provided.

Knitting this level of complexity truly is hard! Get out your stitch markers and a row counter, turn off the TV, and give it a try.

Special Stitches

RIGHT TWIST (RT) K2tog, but do not slip sts from left needle, insert right needle tip between 2 sts just worked and knit the first st again, slip both st off needle (see page 105).

 TIP This maneuver can be awkward, especially for tight knitters. Move the stitches on the left needle closer to the tip and hold them in place with your left thumb or an extra finger so they don't unintentionally slip off. Also, keep the working yarn very loose after working k2tog so you can more easily swing the right needle around to the front to knit the first stitch again. Tighten up the stitches by tugging on the working yarn after you've inserted the right needle into the first stitch on the left needle and be sure to slip both stitches off of the left needle when you're done.

LEFT TWIST (LT) Skip the first st on the left needle, knit the second st through the back loop but do not slip sts from left needle, knit the first st on the left needle in the usual manner, then slip both sts off needle (see page 105).

 TIP The left twist is even more awkward than the right twist, especially the first part where the second stitch is knitted through the back loop, and especially if you knit tightly. Move the stitches on the left needle closer to the tip and hold them in place with your left thumb or an extra finger so they don't unintentionally slip off. Also, keep the working yarn very loose as you knit the second stitch through the back loop so you can more easily swing your right needle around to the front to knit the first

stitch. Tighten up the stitches by tugging on the working yarn after you've inserted the right needle into the first stitch on the left needle and be sure to slip both stitches off of the left needle when you're done.

2/2RC Sl 2 sts onto cn and hold in back, k2, k2 from cn.

 TRANSLATION In this case, 2/2RC is a stockinette-stitch 4-stitch cable in which the 2 stitches on the cable needle are held in the back so that the cable crosses to the right as you face it.

2/2LC Sl 2 sts onto cn and hold in front, k2, k2 from cn.

 TRANSLATION In this case, 2/2LC is a stockinette-stitch 4-stitch cable in which the 2 stitches on the cable needle are held in the front so that the cable crosses to the left as you face it.

4/4 SEED RC Sl 4 sts onto cn and hold in back, work next 4 sts from left needle as k4 or 4 sts in established seed st as they appear, then work 4 sts from cn as k4 or seed st as they appear.

 TRANSLATION This cable involves 8 stitches—4 in stockinette stitch and 4 in seed stitch. The cable maneuver is the same as the previous right-cross cables, but not all of the stitches are knitted. When working this cable, keep the cable stitches in stockinette stitch or seed stitch as established. Sometimes the knit stitches and sometimes the seed stitches will be held on the cable needle.

PROJECT INSTRUCTIONS

CO 40 sts.

ROWS 1–5 Work in k1, p1 seed st as for Basic Cable Square (see page 92).

ROW 6 (WS; set-up row): [P1, k1] 2 times, k1f&b, p2, k2, k1f&b, p4, [k1f&b] 2 times, p5, k1, p1, k1, [k1f&b] 2 times, p4, k1f&b, k2, p2, k1f&b, k2, p1, k1—48 sts.

 TIP After working the set-up row, count the stitches and verify that the knit and purl sequence matches the instructions. This row is especially difficult because the sequences don't make inherent sense. Once this row is established, the others will fall into place.

ROWS 7–51 Keeping first 3 sts and last 3 sts in seed st for border and beg with Row 1 of the individual pattern charts, work center 44 st as foll: 3 sts in rev St st, 2 sts of Right Twist chart, 4 sts in rev St st, 4 sts of 2/2RC chart, 4 sts in rev St st, 8 sts of 4/4Seed RC chart, 4 sts in rev St st, 4 sts of 2/2LC chart, 4 sts in rev St st, 2 sts of Left Twist chart, 3 sts in rev St st.

TIP Row 1 of the individual charts corresponds to Row 7 of the knitting. After working 45 pattern rows (Rows 7–51), you will end with Row 51, which will be Row 1 of the Right Twist, 2/2RC, 2/2LC, and Left Twist charts, and Row 5 of the 4/4Seed RC chart.

+ These instructions truly are hard to follow, even for experienced knitters. To simplify them, you can create your own chart of the center 44 stitches by taping together photocopies of the individual charts, write out the stitch sequence in words for each row, or use stitch and row markers to help you keep your place.

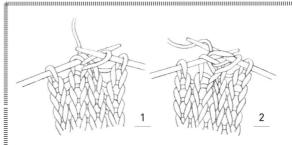

RIGHT TWIST (RT) Knit 2 stitches together but do not slip these stitches from the left needle **(FIGURE 1)**, insert the right needle tip between the 2 stitches just worked and knit the first stitch again **(FIGURE 2)**, then slip both stitches off the needle.

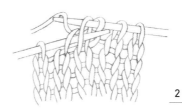

LEFT TWIST (LT) Skip the first stitch on the left needle and knit the second stitch through the back loop **(FIGURE 1)** but do not slip these stitches from the left needle, then knit the first stitch on the left needle as usual **(FIGURE 2)**, then slip both stitches off the needle.

READ YOUR KNITTING Looking at the individual charts and the photograph of the finished square, notice that the first 3 cables and twists on the right-hand side of the square cross to the right, and that the last 2 cross to the left. Okay, that's easy enough to remember (but make a note of it on your pattern if you'd like). Also notice that the right twists and left twists are performed on *every* right-side row, the 4-stitch cables are performed on *every other* right-side row, and the center cable is performed on *every fifth* right-side row. Aha! You can count the twists as you go and use that to tell you where you are in the sequence. You'll make the 4-stitch cables every second time you do the twists, and you'll make the center cable every fifth time you do the twists (does this remind you of Chubby Checker's 1950s hit song?).

TIP Row 1 of the charts (the 7th row of knitting) involves making only the right and left twists. Row 3 involves making both the 4-stitch cables and both twists. The "rev St st" in the instructions tells you that all of these cables and twists are worked against a purl (reverse stockinette stitch) background.

+ Remember that the 4 stitches that begin as seed stitch in the center cable remain as seed stitch regardless of where they appear in the cable.

ROW 52 (WS; DEC ROW) P1, k1, p1, k2tog, k1, p2, k2, k2tog, p4, [k2tog] 2 times, [p1, k1] 2 times, p4, [k2tog] 2 times, p4, k2tog, k2, p2, k1, k2tog, k1, p1, p1, k1—40 sts rem.

ROWS 53–57 Work seed st across all sts as established by seed st side borders.

BO in patt. Weave in ends. Block to measurements.

4/4 SEED RC

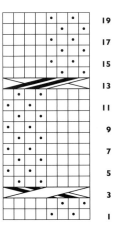

CHART KEY

	k on RS; p on WS
	p on RS; k on WS
	p2tog on RS; k2tog on WS
	k1 f&b
	no stitch

RT (right twist): see instructions

LT (left twist): see instructions

2/2RC: sl 2 sts onto cn and hold in back, k2, k2 from cn

2/2LC: sl 2 sts onto cn and hold in front, k2, k2 from cn

4/4RC knit over seed: sl 4 sts onto cn and hold in back, k4, work [k1, p1] 2 times from cn

4/4RC seed over knit: sl 4 sts onto cn and hold in back, [k1, p1] 2 times k4 from cn

RIGHT TWIST

LEFT TWIST

2/2 RC

2/2 LC

MULTITASKING CABLE

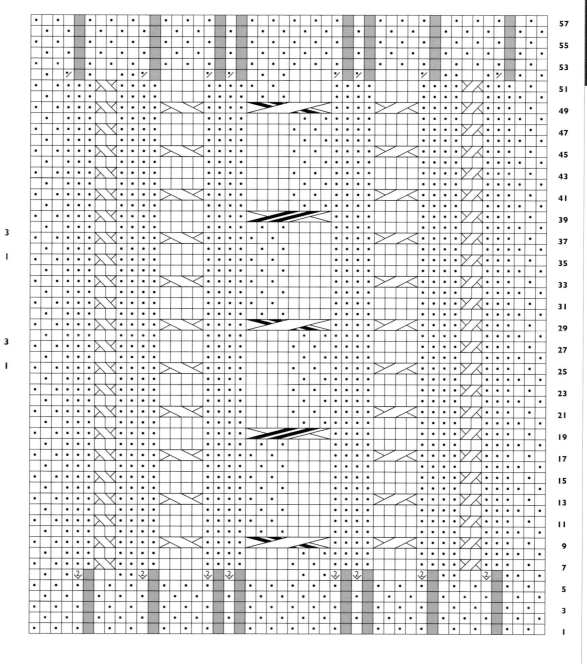

Extra Credit
Plum Tree Square

FINISHED SIZE

About 8" (20.5 cm) square.

MATERIALS

+ Worsted-weight yarn (#4 Medium).

SHOWN HERE Cascade 220 Wool (100% wool; 220 yards [201 meters]/100 grams): #8420 purple.

+ Size U.S. 7 (4.5 mm) needles or size needed to obtain gauge.

+ Cable needle (cn).

+ Tapestry needle.

+ Pins for blocking.

GAUGE

20 stitches and 28 rows = 4" (10 cm); 5 stitches and 7 rows = 1" (2.5 cm) in stockinette stitch, after blocking.

This square combines increases, decreases, cables, and bobbles to create a pictorial design.

This challenging project, based on the Apple Tree pattern from Barbara Walker's *Third Treasury of Knitting Patterns* will help advance your cabling skills. At first glance, it doesn't look like cables are involved because the knitted stitches never cross over each other. However, they do cross over the background purl stitches in a technique called "traveling stitches." But don't be frightened—traveling stitches are formed just like other cables.

This square presents several challenges. The cabling is not performed at a regular or predictable rate, the cables involve either 4 or 2 stitches, some of the stitches are knitted through the back loop, and stitches are increased and decreased to accommodate the pulling in of the cables, but the increases and decreases are not worked on the same rows. In addition, this pattern includes multiple bobbles, which are slow and awkward

to make, but are essential to depict the plums in the tree. A bobble is formed by increasing several stitches into one stitch, then working several rows into those increased stitches by turning the work between rows, then decreasing back to a single stitch. The bobbles in this pattern use yarnovers to increase, and ssk, k2tog, and passing slipped stitches over (psso) to decrease.

Given these challenges, this is the sort of pattern that is best worked by following the chart for each row. This is not mindless, zone-out knitting. But the time and attention are worth it for the spectacular result. If you work this square with relative ease and find it satisfying and magical, you are ready for almost any cable pattern! If you struggle with this square and it brings you to tears, then you may want to stick to regular cables for a while longer.

04

You're out of order!
CABLES AND
CROSSED STITCHES

Special Stitches

2/2RCP Sl 2 sts onto cn and hold in back, k2, p2 from cn.

 TRANSLATION In this case, 2/2RCP is a 4-stitch cable formed with knit and purl stitches in which 2 stitches on the cable needle are held in the back of the work so that the cable crosses to the right.

2/2LCP Sl 2 sts onto cn and hold in front, p2, k2 from cn.

 TRANSLATION In this case, 2/2LCP is a 4-stitch cable formed with knit and purl stitches in which 2 stitches on the cable needle are held in front of the work so that the cable crosses to the left.

1/1RCP Sl 1 st onto cn and hold in back, k1, p1 from cn.

 TRANSLATION In this case, 1/1RCP is a 2-stitch cable formed with knit and purl stitches in which 1 stitch on the cable needle is held in the back of the work so that the cable crosses to the right.

1/1LCP Sl 1 st onto cn and hold in front, p1, k1 from cn.

TRANSLATION In this case, 1/1LCP is a 2-stitch cable formed with knit and purl stitches in which 1 stitch on the cable needle is held in the front of the work so that the cable crosses to the left.

K1TBL K1 through back loop (see page 27).

BOBBLE (K1, yo, k1, yo, k1) in same st, turn work, p5, turn work, ssk, k1, k2tog, turn work, p3, turn work, sl 2, k1, p2sso.

 TRANSLATION This bobble begins by using yarnovers to increase 1 stitch into 5 stitches, then the work is turned and the 5 stitches are purled, then the work is turned again and symmetrical decreases are used to reduce the 5 stitches down to 3 stitches, then the work is turned again and the 3 stitches are purled, and finally, a centered double decrease is used to reduce the 3 stitches back down to 1 stitch.

 TIP Although bobbles are awkward and slow to make, there are only 14(!) of them in this square. Being careful not to work too tightly, insert the right needle into the stitch to be bobbled. Wrap the yarn and pull it through without slipping the stitch off of the left needle, then make a yarnover by bringing the yarn under and over the right needle, knit another stitch (still without slipping the original stitch off of the left needle), make another yarnover, knit 1 more stitch, then slip the original stitch off of the left needle—there will be 5 stitches where there had been just 1. Now turn the work and purl back over these 5 stitches, turn the work again, work a ssk decrease, knit 1 stitch, then knit 2 together— there will now be 3 stitches where there had been 5. Turn the work and purl these 3 stitches, turn the work one more time, slip 2 stitches as if to knit together, knit the last bobble stitch, then pass the 2 slipped stitches over that knitted stitch—only the original bobble stitch remains. On the following row, keep firm tension as you work the stitches adjacent to the bobble to close up any gaps.

✚ The last decrease in this bobble (sl 2, k1, p2sso) is called a centered double decrease. This decrease is formed over 3 stitches, the center of which ends up on top of the other 2. Remember that when slipping stitches in a decrease involving knit stitches, slip the stitches as if to knit, even if this isn't specified in the instructions (and even though it violates the general rule to slip stitches as if to purl). Slipping 2 stitches together as if to knit is the same maneuver that is used at the beginning of a k2tog decrease (which is called a single decrease because just 1 stitch is removed). Knit the next stitch, then use the left needle tip to lift the 2 slipped stitches (now the second and third stitches from the end of the right needle) over the knitted stitch and off the needle. Notice that the center stitch of the 3 just worked lies on top of the other 2, each of which slants toward the center.

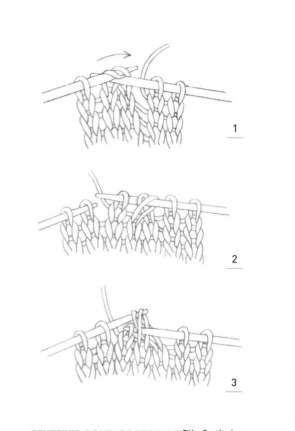

CENTERED DOUBLE DECREASE Slip 2 stitches as if to knit together **(FIGURE 1),** knit the next stitch **(FIGURE 2),** then use the left needle tip to lift the 2 slipped stitches up and over the slipped stitch **(FIGURE 3)**—2 stitches decreased; decrease is vertically aligned.

04

You're out of order!
CABLES AND
CROSSED STITCHES

PROJECT INSTRUCTIONS

CO 40 sts. Work Rows 1–56 of chart. BO in patt. Weave in ends. Block to measurements.

 TIP The names of the cable stitches aren't really necessary to work this pattern. As you read the chart, just notice whether the cable crossing involves 4 or 2 stitches and whether the branch that it is creating needs to cross to the right or left. Keep in mind that in all of these cable crossings, the knit stitches cross over the purl stitches. To accomplish this when the cable leans to the right, the purl stitches are slipped on the cable needle that is held in back of the work; when the cable leans to the left, the knit stitches are slipped onto the cable needle that is held in front of the work. If you forget the verbal instructions for a cable crossing, slip the stitches and manipulate them with your hands to see which direction will give you the correct branch result.

+ The stockinette stitches of the tree are shown shaded lightly in blue for emphasis only. You can color sections of a photocopied chart in this manner to make elements of the design stand out better and make the chart easier to follow.

+ Sometime a cable needle will twist while it is being held in the front or back of the work, which will cause the held stitch(es) to become twisted when worked. To prevent unwanted twisted stitches, always check for the correct stitch mount before you begin working stitches off of the cable needle.

+ Blocking is crucial to create the clear tree shape. The placement of the increases and decreases causes the top of the square to arch instead of lie flat. The tree trunk and branches will act like ribbing and draw in severely. Following the blocking directions on page 31, carefully pin the piece square, then gently pat the bobbles and branches into nice symmetrical shapes.

CHART KEY

☐ k on RS; p on WS

• p on RS; k on WS

k1 tb1 on RS, p1 tb1 on WS

p2tog on RS; k2tog on WS

ssp on RS; ssk on WS

M M1

■ bobble (see instructions)

☐ no stitch

☐ highlight for emphasis (not standard)

1/1RCP (right cross purl): sl 1 st onto cn and hold in back, k1, p1 from cn

1/1LCP (left cross purl): sl 1 st onto cn and hold in front, p1, k1 from cn

2/2RCP: sl 2 sts onto cn and hold in back, k2, p2 from cn

2/2LCP: sl 2 sts onto cn and hold in front, p2, k2 from cn

PLUM TREE

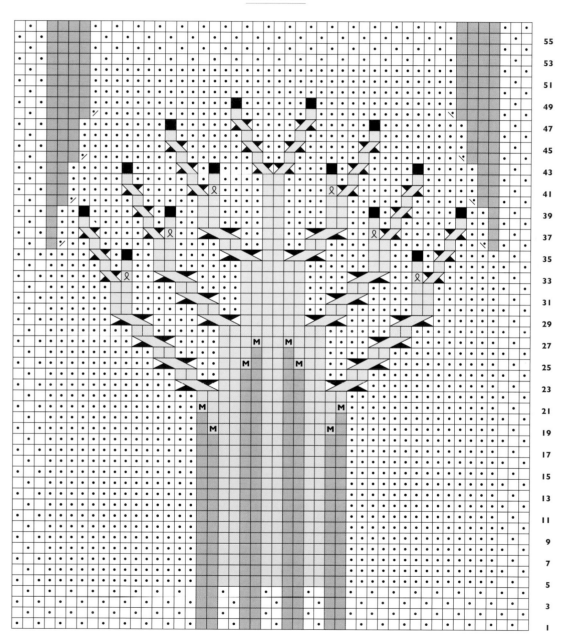

Patchwork Pillow Cover

FINISHED SIZE
About 16" (40.5 cm) square.

MATERIALS
+ Worsted-weight
(#4 Medium) yarn.
SHOWN HERE Berroco Comfort
(50% nylon, 50% acrylic;
210 yards [193 meters]/100
grams): #9701 ivory, #9781
olive, #9721 sprig (light olive),
#9730 teaberry (red),
#9703 barley (tan), and
#9741 bitter sweet (brown),
1 ball each.

+ Size 8 (5cm) needles or size
needed to obtain gauge.

+ Cable needle (cn).

+ 16" (40.5 cm) square
pillow form.

+ Size H/8 (5 mm) crochet hook.

+ 16" (40.5 cm) zipper or hook-
and-loop fastener and matching
sewing thread (optional).

GAUGE
20 stitches and 28 rows = 4"
(10 cm); 5 stitches and 7 rows= 1"
(2.5 cm) in stockinette stitch.

For this project, I crocheted eight squares together to make a cover for a 16" (40.5 cm) pillow form. Crocheted edges can give a polished look to knitted pieces and crochet can be used to join pieces together. I joined these squares with a contrasting color to add a design feature. An alternative to crochet is sewing the squares together with a whipstitch (see page 115). Work the whipstitch in opposite directions for a more decorative seam. Make even more squares and join them into an afghan!

Squares

With red, make two Basic Cable Squares (see page 92). Make two Expanded Basic Cable Squares (see page 98), one with olive and one with tan. With ivory, make two Multitasking Cable Squares (see page 102). Make two Plum Tree Squares (see page 108), one with olive and one with light olive.

Assembly

With wrong sides facing together, pin two squares together along one side edge, easing the fit as necessary. Holding the pinned edge at the top, join brown yarn at the right edge. Insert crochet hook in both squares in rightmost stitch, one stitch in from the edge and draw up a loop. Work single crochet (shown at right) across to join the two squares, easing the fit as necessary.

 TIP Adjust the size and spacing of your crochet stitches as needed to keep the seam flat. When joining the side edges of the squares, try working 1 single crochet stitch in every other knitted row; when joining the top (bind off) and bottom (cast on) edges, try working 1 single crochet stitch in every stitch.

Join three more pairs of squares in the same manner—four pairs of joined squares. Next, hold two of the pairs with wrong sides facing together and pin the bottom edge of one pair to the top edge of the other pair. Join with single crochet to form a four-square panel for the front. Repeat with last two pairs to form the back panel (see the optional directions if you want to create a removable cover). With wrong sides facing together, pin the front and back panels together, easing as necessary to match edges and seams. With the front panel facing you, join brown yarn at the right corner. Work single crochet around three edges, working 3 single crochet stitches in each corner stitch. Insert pillow form. Work single crochet along remaining side.

OPTIONAL **Removable Cover**

Instead of joining together all four squares for the back, leave an opening between the top and bottom two-square pieces. Work 2 rows of single crochet along the top edge of the pair that will form the lower half of the back. Work 4 rows of single crochet along the bottom edge of the pair that will form the top half of the back. With wrong sides facing together, pin the front panel to the back half-panels so that the crocheted edges on the top back half-panel overlaps the bottom half-panel, easing as necessary to match edges and seams. With the front panel facing you, join brown yarn and work single crochet around all four edges, working 3 single crochet stitches in each corner stitch. Handstitch zipper or hook-and-loop fasteners between the two back half-panels.

SINGLE CROCHET (SC) Insert hook into a stitch, yarn over hook and draw through a loop, *insert hook through the next stitch, yarn over hook and draw through another loop, yarn over hook **(FIGURE 1)**, and draw it through both loops on the hook **(FIGURE 2)**. Repeat from * for the desired number of stitches.

WHIPSTITCH SEAM Work whipstitch in opposite directions to form a decorative seam.

TESSELLATED LEAF LACE SQUARE, PAGE 130

05

INTENTIONAL HOLES
LACE AND OPENWORK

The techniques covered in this chapter form the basis for some of the most breathtakingly spectacular knitted items. The purpose of lace knitting is purely decorative; lace knitting emphasizes the aesthetics. Lace is not more durable or warmer than other techniques, but it can be the most beautiful. All weights of yarn can be used for knitting lace but the results are most impressive when the finest yarns are used. Lace knitting is perfect for special-occasion pieces such as wedding shawls and heirloom baby items. If you are awed, as I am, by these exquisite pieces, and think you could never make them, think again!

The patterns grouped under the names of lace and openwork have one thing in common—intentional holes in the fabric made from yarnovers. According to Barbara Walker, the holes are called eyelets when they are separated from each other by more than two strands of yarn; they are called lace when separated by a single strand or two twisted strands. Technically speaking, knitted lace has the yarnovers performed on both right-side and wrong-side rows. Lace knitting, in contrast, has yarnovers worked only on one side of the fabric, with a plain row of knits or purls worked on the other. This classification may be interesting (or not!), but it is not really relevant to you and me as knitters, or to the projects in this chapter. I will use the terms "openwork," "eyelets," and "lace" interchangeably.

As with so much of knitting, the basic technique is remarkably simple: a yarnover hole is paired with a corresponding decrease to keep the stitch count the same—otherwise the yarnover would act as an increase (remember Aunt Liz's and Aunt Nadine's Dishcloth on page 66?). Unending variations from this simple technique are possible.

THE OVERALL BALANCE OF HOLES AND SOLID AREAS, from scattered holes or eyelets against a solid ground, to a fagoting (also spelled faggoting) stitch where the holes are separated by just one or two single strands of yarn.

THE TYPE OF BACKGROUND STITCH, from stockinette stitch to reverse stockinette stitch to garter stitch to a mixture of stitches.

THE DEGREE TO WHICH THE HOLES ALIGN vertically or diagonally throughout the pattern.

THE PROXIMITY OF THE YARNOVERS TO THEIR COMPANION DECREASES, from side by side to several stitches apart.

THE TYPE OF DECREASES USED and whether or not they are mirrored in terms of slant direction.

THE GAUGE at which the pattern is worked, from laceweight to chunky.

THE NUMBER OF STITCHES AND ROWS in the pattern repeat.

Openwork patterns tend to have increased elasticity and stretchiness. They are often worked on larger needles than suggested by the manufacturer (check the yarn bands) to emphasize the openness, and they demand blocking to open up the holes and reveal the pattern. These characteristics have several implications. A gauge swatch is essential when choosing yarn and needles for lace knitting. Don't be surprised if your gauge changes as you get into the rhythm of lace—I tend to loosen up significantly.

Openwork patterns are best worked in natural fibers that block well and hold the blocked shape during use. Be sure to block your gauge swatch because the blocked dimensions are generally much larger than the dimensions of the swatch on the needles. Even if the finished size isn't important, the aesthetic characteristics of your work will vary as your gauge changes, and lace knitting is all about the aesthetics.

A word about tools: because lace knitting involves a large number of manipulations of more than one stitch at a time, you may prefer needles with longer tapers and sharper or more concave points. There are needles made especially for lace knitting. If you find yourself struggling over the stitch operations, try a different type of needle before you give up.

You're likely to find the biggest challenge with lace knitting is keeping track of stitch counts and variations from row to row rather than in the actual stitch manipulations. However, knitting lace in very fine yarn can challenge your eyesight and dexterity as well. It's all the more helpful to know how to read your knitting to avoid mistakes. The projects in this section begin with simple patterns and evolve to more complex patterns. Most of the stitches required—yarnover (yo), knit 2 together (k2tog), and slip, slip, knit (ssk)—were introduced in the Shaping and Cables chapters (see pages 69 and 81). The rest are explained as they come up.

The exercises in this chapter will take you through the basic library of techniques and even get you started working with finer yarn, though not the finest, so you can get your hands (not your feet) wet and decide if you want to try a larger project. You have already worked the most basic of openwork stitches, a yarnover increase in combination with a knit 2 together decrease against a garter-stitch background in Aunt Liz's and Aunt Nadine's Dishcloth.

Tinking Lace: Anticipating and Fixing Mistakes

Although it's possible to fix errors in lace without tinking, it takes quite a bit of confidence and skill, so I recommend tinking if you discover a mistake. Typically, a mistake will throw off the stitch count so you'll notice something is amiss on the very next row. I have found that sometimes I work a k2tog instead of the double decrease, resulting in one extra stitch in the repeat.

There is one mistake you can easily fix without tinking. If you ever realize that you missed a yarnover in the previous row, you can simply pick up the appropriate strand between stitches in the row below from front to back, as you would in the first part of a make-one (M1) increase (see page 78). This picked-up yarnover hole and its neighboring stitches will be slightly smaller than the surrounding stitches (an extra stitch was made from the same length of yarn), but the differences will even out in blocking.

Checkerboard Eyelet Square

FINISHED SIZE

About 8" (20.5 cm) square.

MATERIALS

+ Worsted-weight yarn
(#4 Medium).

SHOWN HERE Cascade 220 Wool
(100% wool; 220 yards
[201 meters]/100 grams):
#2415 dark gold.

+ Size U.S. 7 (4.5 mm)
needles or size needed
to obtain gauge.

+ Tapestry needle.

+ Pins for blocking.

GAUGE

20 stitches and 28 rows = 4"
(10 cm); 5 stitches and 7 rows
= 1" (2.5 cm) in pattern, after
blocking.

Lace is created when yarnover increases are paired with decreases.

Deceptively simple, the eyelets in this design are vertically aligned and arranged in staggered blocks alternating with areas of solid stockinette stitch.

The proportion of holes to solid knitting is just 10 percent. This pattern is based on the Shetland Lace Checkered Acre pattern in Barbara Walker's *First Treasury of Knitting Patterns*.

A couple of things make this square more challenging. First, the pattern is balanced and symmetrical in the square, which means that there are partial repeats at the beginning and end of the rows. This makes it harder to memorize the pattern at first. Also, the design uses slanted decreases (right-slanting k2tog decreases and left-slanting ssk decreases), but it's not easy to tell which one is required by reading the knitting.

Just as with knit-and-purl or cable patterns, lace patterns often include minimal charts that show just one repeat of the pattern stitch. To help you get used to using this type of chart, minimal charts are used here. But don't worry—a larger chart showing the full pattern is also included.

PROJECT INSTRUCTIONS

CO 40 sts.

ROW 1 *K1, p1; rep from * across.

ROW 2 *P1, k1; rep from * across.

ROWS 3 AND 4 Rep Rows 1 and 2.

ROWS 5–12 Keeping the first 4 and last 4 sts in seed st, rep Rows 1 and 2 of Checkerboard Tier 1 chart over center 32 sts 4 times.

ROWS 13–20 Keeping the first 4 and last 4 sts in seed st, rep Row 1 and 2 of Checkerboard Tier 2 chart over center 32 sts 4 times.

 TIP The trick to working any type of pattern stitch is to find the rhythm of the stitches. This rhythm isn't immediately obvious because the Tier 1 chart begins with the second half of the main motif. But notice that the lace motif consists of 6 stitches—2 center stockinette stitches flanked on each side by a yarnover and a decrease that slants toward the center of the motif (a left-slanting ssk decrease at the right edge and a right-slanting k2tog at the left edge). Notice also that the lace motifs are separated by 4 stockinette stitches, which bring the full repeat to 10 stitches wide. The motif is outlined in blue in the large chart, where you can also see why the motif splits across the repeats in the Tier 1 section of the chart (notice how it crosses the red repeat line in the large chart). There are 2 extra unrepeated stitches in the row (at the beginning of the row for the Tier 1 chart and at the end of the row for the Tier 2 chart), which are needed to balance the stitch pattern between the two side edges.

+ Once you understand the structure of the motif, you can work the pattern from memory instead of following the chart stitch by stitch. Your inner dialog for Tier 1 might be "2 extra stitches, left half of motif, 4 knits, full motif, 4 knits, full motif, four knits, right half of motif, 2 knits." For Tier 2, it would be "3 knits, full motif, 4 knits, full motif, 4 knits, full motif, 3 knits." Remember—in this pattern, right-slanting decreases (k2tog) are worked on the left half of the motif; left-slanting decreases (ssk) are worked on the right half of the motif.

+ Check your stitches and stitch count carefully on the first row of a new tier. If the first row is correct, you can check your place in subsequent rows by reading the knitting below.

 READ YOUR KNITTING The lace patterning is all worked on right-side rows; wrong-side rows are simply purled between the seed-stitch borders. Each two-row chart is repeated 4 times vertically in each tier, making each tier in the main chart 8 rows high. You can count the repeats by counting the holes made by the yarnovers. Once there are four holes and you have finished a wrong-side row, you're ready to switch to the other chart.

ROWS 21–52 Rep Rows 5–20 two more times.

ROWS 53–56 Work seed st across all sts as established by seed st side borders.

BO all sts in pattern. Weave in ends. Block to measurements.

CHECKERBOARD TIER 1

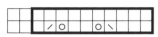

CHECKERBOARD TIER 2

CHECKERBOARD EYELET

55
53
51
49
47
45
43
41
39
37
35
33
31
29
27
25
23
21
19
17
15
13
11
9
7
5
3
1

CHART KEY

☐ k on RS; p on WS

• p on RS; k on WS

╱ k2tog

╲ ssk

○ yo

| outline for emphasis
(not standard)

▢ pattern repeat

Horizontal Sampler Square

FINISHED SIZE

About 8" (20.5 cm) square.

MATERIALS

+ Worsted-weight yarn (#4 Medium).

SHOWN HERE Cascade 220 Wool (100% wool; 220 yards [201 meters]/100 grams): #2415 dark gold.

+ Size U.S. 9 (5.5 mm) needles or size needed to obtain gauge (I used size 10 [6.0 mm] needles because I tend to knit tightly).

+ Two stitch markers.

+ Tapestry needle.

+ Pins for blocking.

GAUGE

15 stitches and 24 rows = 4" (10 cm); 3.75 stitches and 6 rows = 1" (2.5 cm) in Pattern Stitch A, blocked.

Practice making yarnovers before and after decreases and between knit and purl stitches.

This square showcases three stitch patterns in which the density of holes nearly matches the density of the solid areas. You will probably find this easier to work than the Checkerboard Eyelet Square on page 120 because each stitch pattern is worked for several rows in succession, allowing you to become comfortable with the rhythm. The instructions for each pattern are very simple, so no charts are provided. In the upper and lower patterns, yarnovers and decreases are worked on right-side rows only and the wrong-side rows are simply purled. In the center pattern, yarnovers and decreases are worked on both right- and wrong-side rows. This means that you will learn how to make yarnovers between purl stitches and how to decrease while purling. This particular stitch pattern is called fagoting—in the vertical strips, the adjacent holes are separated by just one or two strands of yarn.

Be aware that as you knit, the upper and lower patterns will produce a biased fabric—one that slants. In the lower pattern, which slants to the left, the fabric will bias to the right; in the upper pattern, which slants to the right, the fabric will bias to the left. Biasing occurs when the yarnovers are always on the same side of the companion decreases. The direction of the bias depends on whether the yarnovers are before or after the decreases. The center pattern doesn't bias because the yarnovers and decreases balance out bias directions. Bias effects can usually be eliminated in blocking, so it isn't apparent in the photograph at left.

PROJECT INSTRUCTIONS

CO 29 sts.

? **WHY?** Pattern Stitches A and C each require a multiple of 2 stitches plus 1 (an odd number), Pattern Stitch B requires a multiple of 4 stitches, and the garter-stitch border requires an even number of stitches. Our gauge is 15 stitches per 4" (10 cm), or 30 stitches in 8" (20.5 cm). Therefore, we can allow 25 stitches (an odd number) each for Pattern Stitch A and Pattern Stitch C, and 2 stitches (an even number) of stitches for each border. Voilà, 29 stitches! We can adjust the stitch count of the pattern section to 24 stitches (a multiple of 4) for Pattern Stitch B when the time comes.

TIP Cast on loosely. The stitches in this square will be very elastic, and you will want to stretch them quite a bit while blocking. You'll want to make sure that the cast-on and bound-off edges have the same amount of stretch as the other stitches.

ROW 1 Knit across.

ROW 2 (SET UP ROW) K2, place marker (pm), k25, pm, k2.

? **WHY?** Since there is an extra knit stitch at the end of the rows worked in Pattern Stitch A, the markers will help you verify that the stitch count is correct at the end of these rows, and they will signal you when to switch from knit to purl stitches when you're working the wrong-side rows.

ROWS 3-13 Keeping first 2 and last 2 sts in garter st, work Rows 1–4 of Pattern Stitch A between markers 2 times, then work Rows 1–3 once more.

TIP This pattern stitch is easy to memorize. On the right side, determine if you are working Row 1

or 3 to decide whether to start or end with a k1 (the stitch pattern alternates between beginning with k1 and ending with k1 on right-side rows to create the pattern offset). Then you can get into the easy rhythm of yo, ssk, yo, ssk, etc.

READ YOUR KNITTING Because the yarnovers don't align vertically, how can you tell if you're working this pattern correctly? The easiest way to tell if it's time to work Row 1 or Row 3 is to count the number of vertical holes. The first, third, and fifth holes are made on Row 1; the second, fourth, and sixth holes are made on Row 3. The first stitch slipped for each ssk lines up with the ssk (or beginning k1) in the row below. The second stitch slipped is always above a yarnover. Note that the first slipped stitch ends up on top after the 2 slipped stitches are knit into a decrease.

+ At the end of this sequence of rows (11 rows total and 6 right-side rows of pattern worked), there should be six holes in a diagonal pattern.

ROW 14 Knit across.

? **WHY?** A garter-stitch section separates the pattern sections. It will look best if this garter stitch begins on a wrong-side row so that the purl bumps are visible on the right side. To do this, knit across what would have been Row 4 of Pattern Stitch A.

ROWS 15-17 Knit across.

ROW 18 Knit across, dec 1 st between markers—28 sts rem.

? **WHY?** Pattern Stitch B requires a multiple of 4 stitches, so 1 stitch has to be eliminated. This stitch can be decreased anywhere in the row except in the border stitches where it would disrupt the border pattern. Simply work a k2tog decrease somewhere between the markers in Row 18.

Special Stitches

Pattern Stitch A

(multiple of 2 sts plus 1)

 TRANSLATION When instructions specify a multiple for a pattern stitch, it is providing the information on how many stitches are needed for each full pattern repeat plus the number of additional stitches needed to balance that stitch pattern at the end of the row. This pattern stitch requires a multiple of 2 stitches plus 1 balancing stitch, i.e., any odd number of stitches greater than 1. Knowing the multiple and plus stitches will allow you to vary the width of the fabric as desired—in this case, you can work on any odd number of stitches.

ROW 1 (RS) *Yo, ssk; rep from * to last st, end k1.

ROWS 2 AND 4 P across.

ROW 3 K1, *yo, ssk; rep from * across.

Repeat Rows 1–4 for pattern.

Pattern Stitch B

(multiple of 4 sts)

ROW 1 (RS) *K2, yo, ssk; rep from * across.

ROW 2 *P2, yo, p2tog; rep from * across.

Repeat Rows 1 and 2 for pattern.

Pattern Stitch C

(multiple of 2 sts plus 1)

ROW 1 (RS) *K2tog, yo; rep from * to last st, end k1.

ROWS 2 AND 4 P across.

ROW 3 K1, *k2tog, yo; rep from * across.

Repeat Rows 1–4 for pattern.

 TIP Count the stitches at this point to make sure you have the correct number to begin Pattern Stitch B and to find any hidden mistakes.

ROWS 19–32 Keeping first 2 and last 2 sts in garter st, work Rows 1–2 of Pattern Stitch B between markers 7 times.

 TIP Row 2 of Pattern Stitch B introduces a yarnover between 2 purl stitches. Did that give you pause? Many knitting books will give instructions for performing a yarnover between 2 knits, between a knit and a purl, between a purl and a knit, and between 2 purls, as separate instructions (see page 129). So that you can figure out how to make a yarnover in any situation, it's a good idea to remember two principles. **Principle One:** The yarnover must result in an extra loop on the right needle because it is a form of increase. **Principle Two:** The extra loop must be mounted on the needle the same as the other stitches. In our case, the side of the yarnover loop that's on the front of the needle should be to the right in comparison to the side of the loop that's behind the needle (forming a Z angle instead of an S; see page 28).

+ When making a yarnover after a purl stitch, the yarn is already in the front of the work. Instead of simply moving the yarn between the needles to create the yarnover, we must swing the yarn a full 360° around the right needle—over the top of the needle, then back between the needles to the front where it started.

READ YOUR KNITTING Oh my, there's lots to notice in this pattern. The stitches that are worked plain (knitted or purled) are the decrease stitches and the yarnovers from the previous row. The p2tog is worked on the wrong side—notice that it forms a right-leaning decrease when viewed from the right side of the work. Compare the strands that separate the yarnover holes in Pattern Stitches A and B. The holes in Pattern Stitch B are separated by single interlocking strands; the holes in Pattern Stitch A are separated by two twisted strands.

+ Because we worked seven repeats of the 2-row pattern and because yarnover holes were formed on every row, there should be fourteen holes in each column. The holes will be slightly offset from each other.

ROWS 33–37 Knit across.

ROW 38 Knit across, inc 1 st between markers—29 sts.

WHY? Pattern Stitch C requires an odd number of stitches, so one stitch has to be added. This stitch can be added anywhere in the row except in the border stitches where it would disrupt the border pattern. Simply work the increase of your choice somewhere between the markers in Row 38.

TIP Count the stitches at this point to make sure you have the correct number to begin Pattern Stitch C and to find any hidden mistakes.

ROWS 39–49 Keeping the first 2 and last 2 sts in garter st, work Rows 1–4 of Pattern Stitch C between markers 2 times, then work Rows 1–3 once more.

READ YOUR KNITTING Except for the k2tog decreases that fall at the ends of the pattern, the k2tog decreases in Pattern Stitch C are always worked with the needle inserted into the stitch above the previous decrease first, and into the stitch above the yarnover second. Each new yarnover is 1 stitch to the right of the yarnover hole in the last right-side row.

+ At the end of this sequence of rows (11 rows total and 6 right-side rows of pattern worked), there should be six yarnover holes along a diagonal alignment.

ROWS 50–52 Knit across.

BO all sts loosely. Block to measurements.
Weave in ends.

TIP Bind off loosely. This square will be very elastic, and you will want to stretch it quite a bit during blocking. You'll want the cast-on and bound-off edges to be as stretchy as the rest of the square.

+ When weaving in ends in lace, try to weave them into the solid areas where they will be less visible. Wait until after blocking to trim the ends so that they can stretch along with the rest of the fabric during blocking.

+ Have fun blocking this piece. You will be able to stretch it considerably when it's wet. Notice how you can pin the piece so that the slanted (biased) sides become straight.

YARNOVERS

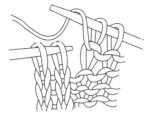

BETWEEN 2 KNIT STITCHES Wrap the yarn around the right needle from front to back—1 stitch increased.

BETWEEN 2 PURL STITCHES Bring the yarn over the top of the right needle (from front to back), then around the bottom of the needle to the front again—1 stitch increased.

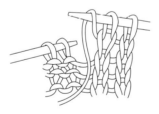

AFTER A KNIT STITCH AND BEFORE A PURL STITCH Bring the yarn to the front under the right needle tip, around the top of the needle to the back, then under the needle again to the front—1 stitch increased.

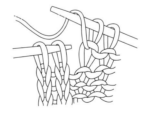

AFTER A PURL STITCH AND BEFORE A KNIT STITCH Bring the yarn over the top of the right needle from front to back—1 stitch increased.

Tessellated Leaf Lace Square

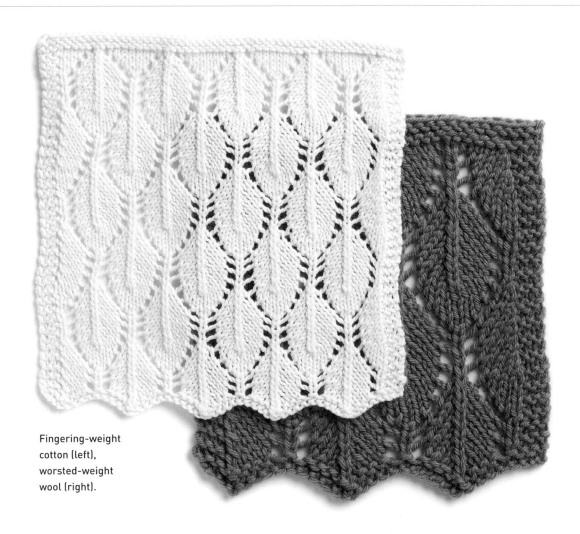

Fingering-weight
cotton (left),
worsted-weight
wool (right).

Lace patterns are formed by strategic placement of increases and decreases while maintaining the same stitch count.

FINISHED SIZE

About 8" (20.5 cm) square at longest point.

NOTE Numbers are given first for worsted-weight yarn followed in parentheses with numbers for fingering-weight yarn. When only one number is given, it applies to both weights.

MATERIALS

+ **WORSTED-WEIGHT YARN** (#4 Medium).

SHOWN HERE Cascade 220 Wool 100% wool; 220 yards [201 meters]/100 grams): #2415 dark gold on size U.S. 9 (5.5 mm) needles or size needed to obtain gauge (I used size 10 [6.0 mm] needles because I tend to knit tightly).

OR

+ **FINGERING-WEIGHT YARN** (#1 Super Fine).

SHOWN HERE Dale of Norway Stork (100% cotton; 195 yards [178 meters]/50 grams): #3 yellow on size U.S. 3 (3.25 mm) needles or size needed to obtain gauge (I used size 4 [3.5 mm] needles because I tend to knit tightly).

+ Tapestry needle.

+ Pins for blocking.

+ Optional: stitch markers.

GAUGE

10 stitches = 2½ (1½)" (6.5 [3.8] cm); 24 rows = 4 (2½)" (10 [6.5] cm) in stitch pattern, after blocking

> **WHY?** Because so many stitches are slanted at an angle, it is more relevant to give the gauge in terms of the size of the pattern repeat, which is 10 stitches wide and 24 rows tall.

This square with its scalloped lower edge, based on the Long Leaf Lace pattern from Barbara Walker's *Fourth Treasury of Knitting Patterns*, displays some of the complex beauty possible with combinations of simple yarnovers and decreases. The word "tessellated" indicates that the surface is covered with identical interlocking shapes without any gaps in between. The Checkerboard Square on page 40 is a simpler tessellated pattern. The shape of an individual leaf is highlighted in blue on the chart.

Three yarnover/decrease maneuvers are used to form the leaves. First, look at the chart on page 133 to notice how most of the yarnovers and decreases are separated by knit stitches. Second, notice that the yarnovers are not aligned vertically but the decreases are. Third, notice that a double decrease is used, which decreases 2 stitches at a time. The yarnovers worked at each side of the leaf are compensated by the single double decrease along the center leaf vein to create a symmetrical leaf. Although the stitch pattern repeats over 24 rows, there are actually two tiers of 12 rows each that are shifted laterally. In fact, each leaf tier is formed from two sets of 6 rows each. The first 6 rows are comprised of three repeats of an easy-to-memorize 2-row sequence. The second 6 rows involve shifting the positions of the yarnovers toward the spine in a regular fashion that requires a bit more attention but is still predictable.

A final complexity: there is a partial pattern repeat at each side edge. Because yarnovers are present for only half a leaf in these partial repeats, they are paired with single decreases instead of the double decreases required in the full pattern repeats.

Why analyze the design in this way? It's not actually necessary, but understanding the structure will help you work the pattern from memory and develop an internal rhythm as you knit. The 24-row, 10-stitch design can be broken down into a simpler inner dialog for each row. For example, Rows 1, 3, and 5 would be, "knit 1 [to start the pattern], yarnover, knit 3, decrease, knit 3, yarnover [leaf finished], knit 1 [to separate the leaves], yarnover, knit 3, decrease, knit 3, yarnover [another leaf completed], knit 1 [another separator], etc."

Special Stitches

CENTERED DOUBLE DECREASE Slip 2 stitches together as if to knit 2 together, knit 1, pass the 2 slipped stitches over the knit stitch.

 TIP This decrease was also used in the Plum Tree bobble (see page 110). Here, it adds a dimensional aspect to the leaves, forming the center vein.

PROJECT INSTRUCTIONS

CO 32 (52) sts. *Note:* Instructions are given first for worsted-weight yarn with fingering-weight yarn in parentheses.

 WHY? The leaf stitch pattern has a 10-stitch repeat. Our worsted-weight square has two full repeats (20 stitches); the fingering-weight square has four full repeats (40 stitches). Another 6 stitches are needed for a partial repeat at the edge (5 stitches for the half leaf plus 1 for the decrease), plus 3 garter stitches at each side for a non-rolling border: 20 (40) stitches + 6 stitches for half repeat + 3 stitches for right border + 3 stitches for left border = 32 (52) stitches.

 TIP Cast on loosely to maintain the elasticity of the lace pattern at the lower edge.

ROWS 1 AND 2 Knit across. Optional: Place a marker 3 stitches in from each end.

Keeping first 3 and last 3 sts in garter st, work Rows 1–24 of chart 1 (2) time(s), then work Rows 1–17 of chart 1 (0) time, then work Rows 1–23 of chart 0 (1) time—43 (73) rows total.

 TRANSLATION Like the "no stitch" symbol (see page 96) on a chart, there is a "no repeat" phrase in these instructions—indicated by "0 times" an action is to be repeated. This is only necessary when a pattern is written for multiple gauges or sizes and a particular instruction does not apply to all of the sizes. In this case, the worsted-weight version requires one full repeat (24 rows) plus one partial repeat of 17 rows to achieve the desired length. The fingering-weight version requires two full repeats (48 rows) plus one partial repeat of 23 rows to achieve the desired length. It will be especially helpful to highlight the numbers that apply to your size on a photocopy of the pattern.

TIP The red line on the chart outlines the pattern repeat, which is an irregular shape in this case. The irregularity accommodates the partial pattern repeats and the shifting position of the decreases in this tessellated pattern. Notice that the stem of a leaf in one tier of leaves serves as the separator between the leaves in the adjacent tier. In Rows 1–12, there is a partial leaf at the left edge of the chart that requires just a single decrease to balance the yarnovers. In Rows 13–24, the partial leaf is shifted to the right edge of the chart, along with the single decrease required to balance the yarnovers. Therefore, the red outline shifts to the left on Rows 13–24 to properly group the yarnovers on each side of a complete leaf with the double decrease, and the single decrease of the partial leaf with its single yarnover.

+ Stop and check the stitches carefully after Row 1 and Row 13 to make sure the pattern is correctly aligned. If you have trouble counting rows, place row markers in the first yarnovers on Row 1 and Row 13 to help keep track.

READ YOUR KNITTING The double decreases always stack up, so the 2 stitches slipped are, from left to right, the stitch directly on top of the previous decrease and the stitch to its right. You can keep track of your place vertically by counting the yarnover holes: the first 6 rows of the pattern create three holes vertically, the next 6 rows create three holes that slant toward the center of the leaf. The holes then are adjacent to the center vein of the neighboring leaf and the position of the elements shifts.

NEXT 3 ROWS Knit across.

BO all sts loosely. Weave in ends. Block to measurements.

CHART KEY

☐	k on RS; p on WS
╱	k2tog
╲	ssk
⋀	sl 2 as if to k2tog, k1, p2sso
O	yo
▨	highlight for emphasis (not standard)
☐	pattern repeat

TESSELLATED LEAF

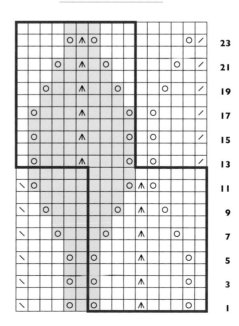

Extra Credit
Leaves and Ladders Square

FINISHED SIZE

About 8" (20.5 cm) square.

MATERIALS

+ Worsted-weight yarn
(#4 Medium).

SHOWN HERE Cascade 220
Wool (100% wool; 220 yards
[201 meters]/100 grams):
#2415 dark gold.

+ Size U.S. 9 (5.5 mm) needles
or size needed to obtain
gauge (I used size 10 [6.0 mm]
needles because I knit tightly).

+ 4 stitch markers.

+ Tapestry needle.

+ Pins for blocking.

GAUGE

Center panel of 15–17 stitches
= 4" (10 cm); 20 rows = 3½"
(9 cm) in Beech Leaf pattern,
after blocking.

Some charts of lace patterns include "no stitch" symbols so that key stitches appear aligned when there is a change in stitch count.

This is the most challenging pattern in the book; it was difficult even for me. But once again, the difficulty is not in forming the stitches but in keeping track of the sequences. Several times I had to rip out a couple of rows because I kept forgetting a yarnover and didn't discover that my stitch count was off until I got to the next right-side row.

The central motif is the Beech Leaf pattern from Barbara Walker's *First Treasury of Knitting Patterns,* which is written out as row-by-row instructions. I decided to chart the pattern here, but notice how little the chart resembles the knitted swatch. In the knitted swatch, the yarnovers that outline the leaf motifs and the purl stitches that form the center "veins" form diagonal patterns, but in the charts on page 137, these yarnovers and purl stitches are aligned vertically. This is because the chart is easier to read if these stitches are stacked vertically, even though they don't appear that way in the knitted square. Furthermore, for the first time in this workbook, the number of stitches in the pattern varies from row to row. In order to align the yarnovers and purl stitches and to accommodate the varying stitch count, a lot of "no stitch"

symbols are required. Another complication is that the wrong-side rows have variations in where the knit and purl stitches occur, which require attention. Also note that sometimes yarnovers are worked before knit stitches and sometimes before purl stitches; remember to wrap the yarn correctly for each (see page 129). And don't overlook the two double decreases—sl 1, k2tog, psso (see page 81) and k3tog (see page 129). The k3tog is used only on Row 9 of the Beech Leaf pattern. Amidst all of this variation, the leaf pattern doesn't become recognizable for several rows so it can be hard to tell if you're working it correctly when you begin.

The "lace ladders" at the right and left edges of the square have extra-large holes that are formed by double yarnovers. At least this pattern is only a 2-row repeat! These larger holes are sometimes used as accents in lace knitting, so it's useful to know how they are worked.

Both the leaves and ladders include mirrored decreases, but the leaf decreases slant away from the center vein, while the ladder decreases slant toward the center of the motif. All of this means that careful counting and constant reference to the chart is essential. As much as I love lace knitting, I don't particularly enjoy this type of pattern because it doesn't allow me to relax into a rhythm. But it is exquisite.

The instructions refer to two minimal charts, one for the leaves and one for the ladders. A more complete chart showing the full width of the piece and two vertical repeats of the 10-row leaf pattern is given for reference. The stitches that form a single leaf shape are shaded in blue. Notice that the complete chart is 35 stitches wide, but the instructions say to cast on just 31 stitches. This is because in the center section two cells of the chart are occupied by yarnovers that represent stitches that will exist after Row 1 has been completed, and two cells contain "no stitch" symbols to maintain the alignment of the other stitches; these "no stitch" symbols occupy space in the chart but do not actually exist in the knitting. Note that the "plus 1" stitch at the left side of the pattern repeat in the minimal Beech Leaf chart appears between the left side of the Beech Leaf pattern repeat and the Lace Ladder repeat in the complete chart.

TIP Make a photocopy of the chart so you can add notes. It's a good idea to highlight the place on Row 3 of the Beech Leaf chart where the yarnovers come before and after a purl stitch so you'll know to pay close attention when forming the yarnovers. Also, highlight the k3tog and sl 1, k2tog, psso decreases in Row 9 and highlight wrong-side Rows 2 and 10, which contain no knit stitches.

PROJECT INSTRUCTIONS

CO 31 sts.

ROW 1 (RS) Knit across.

ROW 2 (WS; SET-UP ROW) K4, pm, k4, pm, k15, pm, k4, pm, k4.

ROW 3 K4, sl marker (sl m), work Row 1 of Lace Ladder chart to next m, sl m, work Row 1 of Beech Leaf chart over center 15 sts, sl m, work Row 1 of Lace Ladders chart to next m, sl m, end k4.

Keeping the first 3 and last 3 st in garter st and the 4th st from each end in St st, cont working Lace Ladder chart as established and at the same time, for the Beech Leaf chart, work Rows 2–10 once, then rep Rows 1–10 two times, then work Rows 1–9 once more, ending with a RS row.

Special Stitches

SL 1, K2TOG, PSSO Slip 1 stitch as if to knit, knit 2 together, pass slipped stitch over the k2tog and off the needle.

 TIP This left-slanting double decrease (see box on page 81) is formed over 3 stitches, the right most of which ends up on top of the other 2.

DOUBLE YARNOVER Wrap the yarn around the right needle two times to form two new loops (see page 139). On the following wrong-side row, purl the first loop and knit the second loop.

TRANSLATION Because the outside border stitches are composed of 3 garter and 1 stockinette stitch, the first 4 and last 4 stitches are always knitted on right-side rows. On wrong-side rows, the first 4 stitches are worked as k3, p1; the last 4 stitches are worked as p1, k3. The 4 stitches adjacent to each border are in the double-yarnover ladder patterns. On right-side rows, work these 4 stitches as ssk, yo, yo, k2tog; on wrong-side rows, work them as p2, k1, p1. Remember that one of the double-yarnover loops is purled and one is knitted. The center stitches are worked according to the 10-row leaf pattern repeat. You will work three complete repeats of this pattern, then work the first 9 rows once more. The tenth row is omitted so that the garter-stitch top border can begin on a wrong-side row, which looks better.

TIP The double yarnovers are worked as p1, k1 on the following wrong-side rows. Purl the first loop, then slip that loop off of the left needle resulting in a very large loop on the left-hand needle. Hold this remaining loop on the needle with a finger, then move the working yarn to the back between the needles, then knit this loop and slip it off the left needle. Move the yarn to the front again to form the next purl stitch.

+ After working another row or 2, look back at the results. The working yarn has been neatly wrapped twice around what looks like a single large yarnover hole. Neat, no?

+ In the center of Row 3 of the Beech Leaf pattern, there is a tricky point where yarnovers are worked on each side of a purl stitch. This uses the same principles as in the Horizontal Sampler on page

---

CHART KEY

☐	k on RS; p on WS	O	yo
•	p on RS; k on WS	▨	no stitch
∕	k2tog	▨	highlight for emphasis (not standard)
＼	ssk	☐	pattern repeat
⅄	sl 1, k2tog, psso		
⫫	k3tog		

LACE LADDER

BEECH LEAF

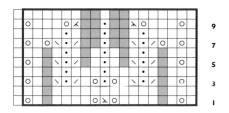

LEAVES AND LADDERS

124: each yarnover must result in an extra loop on the needle (because it is a form of increase), and the extra loop must have the same stitch mount as the rest of the stitches. In this case, the first yarnover is after a knit stitch and before a purl stitch, so the yarn must move completely around the right needle to form the extra loop and be in position for the next purl. But what happens after the purl stitch? Because the following stitch is a knit stitch, as strange as it seems, you don't need to move the yarn at all—just knit the next stitch without moving the yarn to the back between the two needles as you normally would between purl and knit stitches. Instead, bring the yarn over the top of the right needle to get it in position to knit the next stitch—this will form the yarnover.

NEXT ROW (WS) Removing markers as you come to them, knit to first marker, k1, p1, k2, knit to next marker, k1, p1, k2, knit to end.

 TRANSLATION Knit every stitch in this row except purl the first stitch of each double yarnover. This wrong-side row establishes the garter-stitch border while maintaining the double yarnover twists as before. The markers aren't needed in the garter-stitch border.

NEXT 2 ROWS Knit across.

BO all sts loosely. Weave in ends. Block to measurements.

 TIP The stitch pattern produces a pronounced curve along the top (bind-off) and bottom (cast-on) edges, which you will want to emphasize in the blocking.

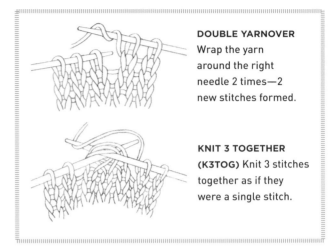

DOUBLE YARNOVER Wrap the yarn around the right needle 2 times—2 new stitches formed.

KNIT 3 TOGETHER (K3TOG) Knit 3 stitches together as if they were a single stitch.

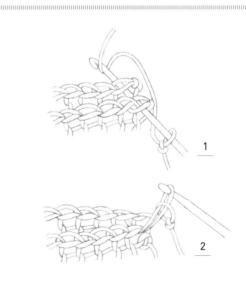

SLIP-STITCH CROCHET SEAM With right sides facing together and working 1 stitch at a time, *insert crochet hook through both thicknesses into the stitch just below the edge, yarn over hook **(FIGURE 1)**, and draw this loop through both thicknesses, then through the loop on the hook **(FIGURE 2)**. Repeat from *, keeping even tension on the crochet stitches.

DIY Scarf

Many of the sample squares in this book can be knitted longer to make a scarf, particularly the Checkerboard Square (page 40), Basic Cable Square (page 92), Expanded Basic Cable Square (page 98), Multitasking Cable Square (page 102), the center pattern (the upper and lower patterns will create biased fabric) from the Horizontal Sampler Square (page 124), Tessellated Leaf Lace Square (page 130), and Leaves and Ladders Square (page 134).

If you like the yarn, gauge, and the finished width of the sample square, merely cast on the same number of stitches, work the lower border, then knit the pattern stitch to desired length, ending with a completed pattern—a tier of blocks, or a cable or lace pattern repeat. Finish it off by working the upper border.

The "desired length" varies by style and personal preference. In general, 60" (152.5 cm) is a good length for a scarf. This length will require about 400 yards of worsted-weight (#4 Medium) yarn, and will allow for some fringe. More yarn will be needed for a longer scarf or a pattern that involves cables; less yarn will be needed for lace patterns.

Note that the Tessellated Leaf Lace and Leaves and Ladders patterns (pages 130 and 134, respectively) are not vertically symmetrical. If you use one of these patterns, you'll have to work the scarf in two halves if both ends of the scarf are to look the same. Work two identical pieces, each half the desired finished length, ending with a garter-stitch border at the top. Then join the two halves with a backstitch or slip-stitch crochet seam (at right). There are more invisible ways to join the two halves by using a provisional cast-on or by grafting, but these advanced techniques are not covered in this workbook.

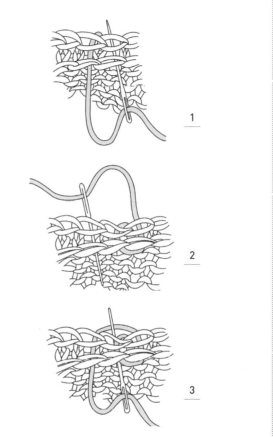

BACKSTITCH SEAM Pin pieces to be seamed with right sides facing together. Working from right to left into the edge stitch, bring the threaded needle up between the next 2 stitches on each piece of knitted fabric, then back down through both layers, 1 stitch to the right of the starting point **(FIGURE 1)**. *Bring the needle up through both layers a stitch to the left of the backstitch just made **(FIGURE 2)**, then back down to the right, through the same hole used before **(FIGURE 3)**. Repeat from *, working backward 1 stitch for every 2 stitches worked forward.

BASIC CABLE UNISEX HAT, PAGE 148

06

GOING IN CIRCLES
KNITTING IN ROUNDS

Up to this point, all of the swatches have been knitted back and forth in rows, also called "knitting flat." However, anything that has a tubular shape—hats, socks, bags, sleeves—can be knitted circularly, also called "knitting in the round," to eliminate the need for seams.

Circular knitting progresses in a spiral and the instructions refer to rounds instead of rows. To keep track of where one round ends and the next begins, a stitch marker is usually placed on the needle between the last stitch of one round and the first stitch of the next.

In circular knitting, the same side of the work—most commonly designated the "right" side—is always facing you. Therefore, stockinette stitch is worked by knitting every stitch of every round (no purling!), and garter stitch is worked by alternating a round of knit stitches with a round of purl stitches.

In circular knitting, the stitches are held with a circular needle, which is nothing more than two straight needles connected by a flexible cable. Circular needles come in various lengths to accommodate different numbers of stitches. When there are too few stitches to fit comfortably around a circular needle, four or five double-pointed needles are used instead.

Step Around Pillow Cover

Learn to knit in the round with a short circular needle, which many knitters find easier than double-pointed needles.

FINISHED SIZE

About 16" (40.5 cm) wide and 12" (30.5 cm) tall, buttoned.

MATERIALS

+ Super bulky yarn (#6 Super Bulky).
SHOWN HERE Lion Brand Wool-Ease Thick & Quick (86% acrylic, 10% wool, 4% rayon, 108 yards [98 meters]/170 grams) #402 wheat, 2 balls.

NOTE Less than 5 yards (5 meters) of yarn remained from the second ball; you might want to purchase a third ball for ensurance.

+ Size U.S. 13 (9 mm) 24" (60 cm) circular needle, or size needed to obtain gauge and one extra needle in same size for three-needle bind-off.

+ Size 12" × 16" (30.5 × 40.5 cm) knife-edge rectangular pillow form (available at fabric and craft stores).

+ Three 1¼" to 1½" (3.2 to 3.8 cm) buttons.

+ Tapestry needle.

+ Pins for blocking.

GAUGE

10 stitches and 16 rows or rounds = 4" (10 cm) in stockinette stitch.

This pillow cover is knitted in a single piece, beginning with the flap that is worked back and forth in rows and shaped by casting on in a series of steps. Buttonholes are worked in this section. At the end of the flap, additional stitches are cast on to accommodate the full pillow circumference, then the stitches are joined into a circle (or "round") and worked to the desired length, ending with a three-needle bind-off.

Beginning knitters often believe that very thick yarn will be easier and faster to work with than a fine yarn. This project gives you a chance to test this idea. Personally, I find that thick yarns cause more hand and finger fatigue because they require larger movements. But I wanted to introduce circular knitting by working with a circular needle instead of four (or five) double-pointed needles, which require much more manual dexterity. At a gauge of 2.5 stitches to the inch, the number of stitches required for this pillow cover can easily fit around a 24" (60 cm) circular needle, which I find the easiest size to knit with. A thinner yarn would require more stitches to fit comfortably around a 24" (60 cm) circular needle, and would take longer to knit.

PROJECT INSTRUCTIONS

Pillow Flap

CO 14 sts.

ROWS 1 (WS) AND 2 (RS) Knit across.

ROW 3 (WS) K2, p10, k2.

ROW 4 (RS; FIRST ROW OF BUTTONHOLE) K6, BO 2 sts (1 st rem on right needle after BO), k5.

 WHY? Binding off 2 stitches requires working 3 stitches (knit 2, slip 1 stitch over the other and off the needle, knit the third stitch, and then slip the second stitch over the third and off the needle), so there is 1 fewer stitch to work after the last bind-off at the end of row if the buttonhole is centered.

ROW 5 (SECOND ROW OF BUTTONHOLE) K2, p4, use the backward-loop method (see at right) to CO 2 sts, p4, k2.

 WHY? The backward-loop cast-on adds loops to the left of the stitches on the right-hand needle, which is what we need to compensate for the bound-off stitches.

ROWS 6–8 Work even, keeping the first 2 and last 2 sts in garter st and the center 10 sts in St st.

ROW 9 (WS) Using the cable method (see page 60), CO 14 st at beg of row, then beg with the newly CO sts, k16, p10, k2—28 sts.

WHY? This set of cast-on stitches will form the second (center) step in the flap. The cable cast-on method adds stitches to the right of the stitches on the left-hand needle, which is why these stitches are added at the start of a wrong-side row. After the stitches are cast on, they become the first stitches worked in this row.

Two-Row Buttonholes

This buttonhole accommodates buttons 1" to 1½" (2.5 to 3.8 cm) in diameter when worked in a super bulky yarn. Reduce or increase the number of stitches bound off in Row 1 to accommodate different button sizes, making the same change to the number of stitches cast on in Row 2.

ROW 1 Work to desired buttonhole position, BO 2 stitches, work to end of row.

ROW 2 Work to gap formed by BO on previous row, use the backward-loop method (see page 145) to CO 2 sts over the gap to complete the buttonhole, work to end.

This simple pillow project combines casting on in a series of steps, buttonholes, and knitting in rounds.

ROW 10 Knit across.

ROW 11 K2, p24, k2.

ROW 12 (FIRST ROW OF BUTTONHOLE) K20,
BO 2 sts, k5.

ROW 13 (SECOND ROW OF BUTTONHOLE) K2, p4,
use the backward-loop method to CO 2 sts, purl to last
2 sts, k2.

ROWS 14–16 Work even, keeping the first 2 and last 2 sts
in garter st and the center 24 sts in St st.

ROW 17 Using the cable method, CO 14 st at beg of row,
then beg with the newly CO sts, k16, p24, k2—42 sts.

ROW 18 Knit across.

ROW 19 K2, p38, k2.

ROW 20 (FIRST ROW OF BUTTONHOLE) K34,
BO 2 sts, k5.

ROW 21 (SECOND ROW OF BUTTONHOLE) K2, p4, use
the backward-loop method to CO 2 sts, purl to last 2 sts, k2.

ROW 22 Knit across.

ROW 23 K2, p38, k2.

ROWS 24, 25, AND 26 Knit across.

Make sure that the stitches are not twisted around the needle (they are twisted here) when you join for working in rounds.

BACKWARD-LOOP CAST-ON *Loop the working
yarn and place it on the needle backward so that
it doesn't unwind. Repeat from *.

Pillow Body

Using the backward-loop method, CO 42 sts—84 sts.

? **WHY?** This cast-on method produces an edge that isn't very stable or pretty, but it will be hidden under the flap. This method is fast to work, and it allows stitches to be added at the left-hand end of the row, so that the working yarn is where it's needed to begin working in rounds.

Place marker (pm) for beg of rnd and, being careful not to twist the stitches, join for working in rnds by purling the first st on the left needle tip.

? **WHY?** The easiest way to join the stitches into a circle is to just start working them. Make sure the right side of the piece is facing outward (toward you) and that the working yarn is on the needle tip in your right hand. Place a stitch marker on the right needle to indicate where the rounds begin and end. Purl the first stitch on the left needle tip. The first round is purled to set up the garter-stitch pattern.

TIP Arrange the stitches so that all of the loops are along the inside of the circle formed by the needle and all of the cast-on bumps are along the outside of the circle.

Beg with a purl rnd, work 4 rnds in garter st (alternate purl 1 rnd, knit 1 rnd).

TIP If you find that the backward-loop cast-on stitches are tight on the needle and difficult to purl, slide them to the tapered point of the needle where there will be more slack.

   + If you drop one of the cast-on stitches, re-form the loop with your fingers and slip it back onto the left needle tip.

Continue in St st (knit every rnd) until piece measures 12" (30.5 cm) from beg of pillow body.

TIP At some point, you will need to join a new ball of yarn. This is best done at a side edge so that the tails of yarn can be hidden along the selvedge. However, when working in rounds there is no side edge. To make the join as invisible as possible, join the new ball to the back of the pillow body (the part that is connected to the flap), even if it means joining before you've reached the very end of the first ball of yarn. There are (of course) many ways to join yarn. In this case, I suggest you make a slipknot a few inches from the end of the new ball and attach it to the end of the old ball. Slide the slipknot up close to your needles and start knitting with the new ball. You'll untie this slipknot and weave in the ends during the finishing process.

READ YOUR KNITTING After knitting a few inches, stop and compare the gauge in the body, which was knitted in rounds, with the gauge in the flap, which was knitted flat. The two may differ because the body involves just knit stitches while the flap includes both knit and purl stitches. This is a good example of why it is important to make a gauge swatch in the round for projects that will be knitted in the round.

Work 4 rnds in garter st (alternate purl 1 rnd, knit 1 rnd).

With WS facing tog, use the three-needle method (see page 147) to BO all sts.

TIP Fold the circular needle in half so that the two points are in your left hand, 42 stitches are on each needle tip, the wrong sides are facing together (right sides facing outward), and the working yarn is attached to the stitches on the needle farthest from you. Typically, this type of bind-off is worked with the right sides of the piece facing together so that the seam ridge is on the wrong side of the piece.

However, for this project, the bind-off edge forms a decorative ridge on the right side of the piece.

+ The number of stitches should match on the two needles, but if you have single stitch left over on one of the left needles at the end, don't panic. Just bind it off as usual.

Weave in ends. Block pillow flap and garter-stitch border of pillow body.

? **WHY?** The body of the pillow may not need blocking because once the pillow form is inserted, it will smooth out the body and the bind-off row will keep the bottom edge straight. However, the backward-loop cast-on is not very stable and the flap will look better after it's been blocked.

TIP When weaving in ends, untie the slipknot from where a new ball was joined and weave in each end separately in the direction it would have gone if you had been knitting with it. This will prevent holes.

+ I blocked my pillow by rolling the flap and garter-stitch top part of the body in a wet towel and letting it set for a few minutes to get damp. Then I pinned out the flap with its right side facing up and the garter top border between the flap and the body pinned straight across and allowed it to dry completely before removing the pins.

Insert pillow form, fold flap over body, and mark placement of buttons under buttonholes. Remove pillow form and sew buttons in place.

TIP Depending on the size of the holes in the buttons, you can sew them to the pillow with the yarn used for knitting or with matching sewing thread. Buttons with shanks can be attached either way. In general, it looks better if buttons with holes are attached with yarn than with sewing thread.

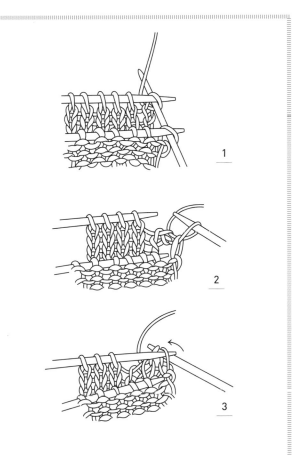

THREE-NEEDLE BIND-OFF Place the stitches to be joined onto two separate needles and hold the needles parallel (shown here with the right sides of the knitting facing together). Insert a third needle into the first stitch on each of the two needles **(FIGURE 1)** and knit them together as if there were a single stitch **(FIGURE 2)**, *knit the next stitch on each needle the same way, then use the left needle tip to lift the first stitch over the second and off the needle **(FIGURE 3)**. Repeat from * until no stitches remain on the first two needles. Cut the yarn and pull the tail through the last stitch to secure.

Basic Cable Unisex Hat and Scarf

Learn to use double-pointed needles (and
practice cables and decreases) in a simple hat.

FINISHED SIZE

About 18¼" (46.5 cm)
around and 8½" (21.5 cm)
tall, excluding pom-pom.
Hat comfortably stretches to
fit a 21" to 22" (53.5 to 56 cm)
diameter head.

MATERIALS

+ Bulky-weight yarn
(#5 Bulky).
SHOWN HERE Berroco Peruvia
Quick (100% wool; 103 yards
[94 meters]/100 grams):
#9145 azul (blue heather)
or Misti Alpaca Chunky
(100% baby alpaca; 108 yards
[97 meters]/100 grams):
#9100 lavender, 1 skein.

+ Size U.S. 10½ (6.5 mm):
set of 5 double-pointed (dpn),
or size needed to obtain
gauge.

+ Cable needle (cn).

+ Size N/15 (10 mm)
crochet hook for adding
fringe to scarf; optional.

+ Pom-pom maker or
cardboard for making
pom-pom; optional.

+ Tapestry needle.

GAUGE

14 stitches and 18 rows
or rounds = 4" (10 cm)
in cable pattern, after
blocking.

NOTE For a snugger fit,
work the ribbing with
a smaller needle.

I love working with double-pointed needles
(abbreviated "dpn"s), but I think this puts me
in a minority of knitters. Recently knitters
have designed ways to work with two circular
needles or one extra-long circular needle to
substitute for double-pointed needles, but being
able to manage double-points is a valuable
knitting skill.

This simple hat is worked in the round on five
double-pointed needles.

It's possible to work the lower portion of the hat
with a short circular needle, but when decreases
are worked to shape the top, there will be too few
stitches to fit around a circular needle, and you'll
need to change to double-pointed needles. In
contrast, the same double-points can be used for
the entire hat—no needle changing required.

Double-pointed needles come in sets of four or
five needles, but you actually knit with just two
needles at a time. The remaining needles sit in
a circle or polygon, holding the other stitches
until it is their turn to be worked. The difficulty
is that the remaining needles sitting there, in a
circle or polygon, get in your way!

When four needles are used, the stitches are divided among three needles and the fourth is used for knitting. When five needles are used, the stitches are divided among four needles and the fifth is used for knitting. You'll need to discover how your hands want to hold all of the needles—there is no right or wrong way. I like to rest the needles not in use between the fingers that are not involved in manipulating the two working needles. The first few rounds are the hardest to manage. After that the fabric helps to stabilize the needles and yarn, and the knitting becomes much easier to manage—so don't give up too soon.

It is not uncommon for "ladders" of loose stitches to occur at the boundaries between the needles. These ladders are formed by relatively long horizontal strands between the last stitch on one needle and the first stitch on the next. To prevent ladders, pay close attention when you move from one needle to the next and work the first couple of stitches on each needle tightly. Eventually, you'll learn to do this by feel without thinking.

For this project, five needles are specified, which allows the stitches to be evenly divided among four needles. But in fact, there's no rule that says you have to use four or five needles—you decide what works for you.

After the bottom ribbing, the hat is worked from a chart. When working in the round, in which the right (or "public") side is always facing out, every chart round is worked from right to left. No boustrophedon here, as the ox can be thought of as going uphill in a spiral instead of back and forth in a flat field. The rounds are all numbered on the right-hand side of the chart for this reason. The chart includes one repeat of the pattern, which will be worked eight times in each round.

The hat pattern includes three types of decreases, each chosen for a particular reason. The p2tog decrease is nearly invisible in the reverse stockinette sections. The ssk decrease slants to the left and hides a purl stitch under a knit stitch. The k3tog double decrease maintains the same slant as the cable crosses.

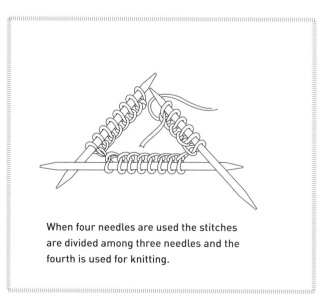

When four needles are used the stitches are divided among three needles and the fourth is used for knitting.

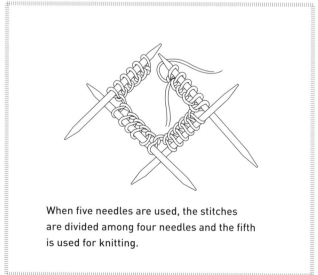

When five needles are used, the stitches are divided among four needles and the fifth is used for knitting.

Hat

PROJECT INSTRUCTIONS

CO 64 sts. Arrange sts evenly on four dpns. Place marker (pm) for beg of rnd and join, being careful not to twist stitches.

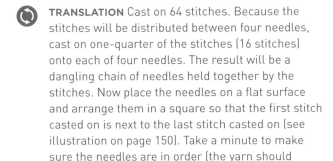 **TRANSLATION** Cast on 64 stitches. Because the stitches will be distributed between four needles, cast on one-quarter of the stitches (16 stitches) onto each of four needles. The result will be a dangling chain of needles held together by the stitches. Now place the needles on a flat surface and arrange them in a square so that the first stitch casted on is next to the last stitch casted on (see illustration on page 150). Take a minute to make sure the needles are in order (the yarn should travel straight from one needle to the next) and that the stitches are not twisted on the needles (all of the loops should be along the inside of the square).

TIP By convention, the needle that contains the first stitches cast on is designated Needle 1; the needle that contains the last stitches cast on (the working yarn is attached to this needle) is designated Needle 4. The other needles are designated (can you guess?) Needle 2 and Needle 3. Arrange the needles so that Needle 4 is on the right-hand side. Pick up the fifth needle in your left hand and join into a round by knitting the stitches on Needle 1. You will work with these two needles (Needle 1 and the fifth working needle) just as if you were working back and forth—ignore the other three needles as much as possible.

+ Pull the yarn very snugly when you knit the first stitch to close the gap between Needle 1 and Needle 4.

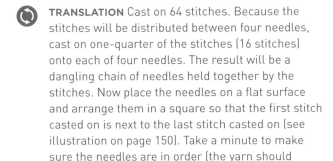 **TRANSLATION** A stitch marker is necessary to denote the boundary between the end of one round and the beginning of the next. However, you will

Note

I used size 11 (8 mm) needles for the blue hat and scarf because I tend to knit tightly. My friend Joanne, who is not a tight knitter, knitted the lavender hat. She used size 9 (5.5 mm) needles for the ribbing and size 11 (8 mm) for the cable portion of the hat. The alpaca yarn has less body and resilience than the wool, and Joanne's ribbing was not snug enough when she used size 11 (8 mm) needles. Also, Joanne's head is smaller than mine. We worked out the needle sizes by swatching both the ribbing and the cable pattern before casting on for the hat itself. The recommended needle size given for this pattern is the one recommended by the manufacturer for the wool yarn I used. To make sure your hat will fit, swatch with different size needles. Although it's recommended that you work your swatch using the same method you'll use for the project (flat or in the round), for this project, you can get by with knitting your swatches flat.

quickly discover that a stitch marker will not stay on the end of a double-pointed needle. Instead of placing a stitch marker on the needle, you can let the tail from the cast-on serve as an indicator for the beginning (or end) of the round. Another option is to rearrange the stitches slightly so that the first stitch of the round is the second stitch on Needle 1. That way, the marker is between the first 2 stitches on Needle 1. Yet another option is to place the marker between the last 2 stitches on Needle 4. Most published instructions will tell you to add a marker to denote the end or beginning of the round—you can decide whether or not it's necessary for a particular project.

 TIP I like to join for working in rounds by changing position of the first and last stitches casted on.

I slip the last cast-on stitch onto the beginning of Needle 1, then lift the first cast-on stitch over that stitch and onto the end of Needle 4. This is a bit awkward to do at first, but it creates an invisible join. You can remember this method by a verse from Matthew (20:16): "So the last shall be first, and the first last . . ."

Work in k1, p1, ribbing for 2" (5 cm).

 TIP To prevent stitches from unintentionally falling off the needles not in use, push the stitches to the center of the needles.

Work Rnds 1–28 of Hat chart, rep the 8 st patt 8 times around on each rnd—8 sts rem after Rnd 28.

Cut yarn leaving a 12" (30.5 cm) tail. Thread tail on a tapestry needle, pull it through the rem sts, pull tight to close hole, and fasten off on WS. Block if desired. Optional: Make a 1½ " (3.8 cm) pom-pom (see below) and attach to top of hat.

 TIP Hats are best blocked over a curved surface rather than laid flat. After dampening the hat, I created a ball-shaped form by stuffing a plastic bag with other plastic bags, then placed the form inside the hat and set the bottom of the form in a bowl with a smaller diameter than the hat. This elevated the hat and allowed the ribbing to stay compressed and the top of the hat to take on a domed shape.

Pom-Pom

Cut stiff cardboard or other material into a template about 3" (7.5 cm) wide. Wrap yarn around template the desired times (75 times for the pom-pom shown here). Carefully slip the wraps off of the template and tie them together tightly and securely in the center, leaving long enough yarn tails to use to attach the pom-pom to the top of the hat. Cut the loops, shake to fluff ends, and trim.

TIP You can make a pom-pom of the size and fullness you want. We actually made three pom-poms, one too small and one too large, before making one that was just right for this hat. The number of wraps needed will vary with the thickness of the yarn and the desired fullness. The alpaca yarn we used was lofty but not too substantial, so 75 wraps were needed to give the fullness we wanted. Your mileage may vary.

HAT

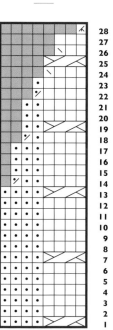

CHART KEY

- knit
- • purl
- ＼ ssk
- ⋎ p2tog
- 人 k3tog
- no stitch

2/2RC: sl 2 sts onto cn and hold in back, k2, k2 from cn

Scarf

Knit a matching scarf (worked back and forth in rows) to go with your hat. The scarves shown measure about 8" (20.5 cm) wide and 60" (152.5 cm) long, excluding fringe, and require 3 skeins of the hat yarn.

NOTE If you want to add optional fringe, cut 60 lengths of yarn, each 14" (35.5 cm) long and set side before casting on stitches for the scarf.

PROJECT INSTRUCTIONS

CO 28 sts. Knit 2 rows. Rep Rows 1–6 of Scarf chart until piece measures about 60" (152.5 cm) from CO, or desired length. Knit 2 rows.

BO. Block or steam-press lightly.

OPTIONAL **Fringe**

Mark placement for five fringe bundles evenly spaced across each short end. Attach a six-strand bundle of precut fringe at each marked location as foll: With wrong-side of scarf facing, insert crochet hook from front to back (from wrong side to right side) one row from up from scarf end, fold six pre-cut fringe strands in half over crochet hook, use hook to pull the strands through to wrong side, insert the ends of the strands through the loop created, and tighten to secure in place. Trim fringe lengths even.

SCARF

Final Exam
Enchanted Cottage Pillow

FINISHED SIZE

Appliqué measures about
11½" (29 cm) wide and
9¾" (25 cm) tall.

MATERIALS

+ Worsted-weight
(#4 Medium) yarn.
SHOWN HERE Berroco Comfort
(50% nylon, 50% acrylic;
210 yards [193 meters]/100
grams): #9720 hummus, 1 ball.

+ Size 8 (5 mm) needles or
size needed to obtain gauge.

+ Cable needle (cn).

+ Tapestry needle.

+ A few yards (meters) of brown
yarn for attaching appliqué.

+ 20" (51 cm) square pillow.

GAUGE

20 stitches and 28 rows = 4"
(10 cm); 5 stitches and 7 rows =
1" (2.5 cm) in stockinette stitch).

This design, from Barbara Walker's *Second Treasury of Knitting Patterns*, is called "Enchanted Cottage." It includes a little bit of everything—knit-and-purl textures, lace, cables, and two large purled bobbles. This is a fitting piece to show off your depth of knitting skill.

Most of the cables in this piece involve an uneven number of stitches, with 2 stitches crossing over a single stitch in order to travel across the background. In the cables that define the window and door, the single stitch is knitted. In the cables that define the roof, the single stitch is purled because it is incorporated into the reverse stockinette background, except for the chimney, which begins on Row 59 where the single stitch is knitted. At the top of the roof beginning in Row 69, the single stitch becomes 2 stitches and the cables are worked over 3 stitches that cross 2 over 2. The result is that the top of the roof has a more rounded shape. (TIP The tricky parts in Rows 59 and 69 of the chart have been highlighted in blue so you don't miss them.)

PROJECT INSTRUCTIONS

Appliqué Square

CO 60 sts.

Work Rows 1–82 of Enchanted Cottage chart.

BO knitwise. Weave in ends. Block to measurements.

Assembly

With dark brown yarn, use a blanket stitch (see page 156) to appliqué cottage to center of purchased pillow. If the pillow fabric is tightly woven, you may need to use embroidery floss and a sharp-point sewing needle. For variation, try a different stitch for the appliqué or embroider a few flowers in the front yard of the cottage or a vine around the door.

Special Stitches

2/1 RC Sl 1 st onto cn and hold in back, k2, k1 from cn.

2/1 RCP Sl 1 st onto cn and hold in back, k2, p1 from cn.

2/2 RCP Sl 2 sts onto cn and hold in back, k2, p2 from cn.

2/1 LC Sl 2 sts onto cn and hold in front, k1, k2 from cn.

2/1 LCP Sl 2 sts onto cn and hold in front, p1, k2 from cn.

2/2 LCP Sl 2 sts onto cn and hold in front, p2, k2 from cn

 TRANSLATION For this pattern, the cable maneuvers have been named based on the number of stitches, the direction of the cross, and whether or not purl stitches are involved. The first number indicates the number of stitches that will be on top of the cable crossing and the second number indicates the number of stitches over which the top stitches cross. "R" indicates a right cross, "L" indicates a left cross, and "P" indicates that purl stitches are involved.

LARGE PURL BOBBLE ([K1, yo] 3 times, k1) all in the same st, turn work, k7, turn work, p7, turn work, k2, sl 1, k2tog, psso, k2, turn work, p5, turn work, k1, sl 1, k2tog, psso, k1, turn work, p3tog.

 TRANSLATION This bobble begins like the one on page 110 by alternating knits and yarnovers, but in this case a single stitch is increased to 7 stitches to make a large bobble. Another difference is that the stitches are purled on right-side rows and knitted on wrong-side rows so that reverse stockinette stitch appears on the public side, giving the bobble extra texture. The decreases are worked on 3 of the 7 rows.

DOUBLE YARNOVER Wrap the yarn twice around the needle. On the subsequent row, work these two loops as k1, p1.

 TIP The double yarnovers in the Leaves and Ladders Square (page 134) were worked as p1, k1 on subsequent rows. It doesn't matter which order the 2 stitches are worked as long as one loop is knitted and the other is purled.

CHART KEY

☐	k on RS; p on WS
•	p on RS; k on WS
୧	p1 tb1 on WS
/	k2tog
\	ssk

BLANKET-STITCH APPLIQUÉ
Working from left to right, bring threaded needle in and out of both layers (the piece to be appliquéd and the background), always keeping the needle on top of the yarn.

Legend

λ	sl 1, k2tog, psso
Λ	sl 2 as if to k2tog, k1, p2sso
⼊	k3tog
O	yo
⊡	purl bobble or large purl bobble
▢	highlight for emphasis (not standard)
O O	double yarnover
2/1RC	sl 1 st onto cn and hold in back, k2, k1 from cn
2/1LC	sl 2 sts onto cn and hold in front, k1, k2 from cn
2/1RCP	sl 1 st onto cn and hold in back, k2, p1 from cn
2/1LCP	sl 2 sts onto cn and hold in front, p1, k2 from cn
2/2RCP	sl 2 sts onto cn and hold in back, k2, p2 from cn
2/2LCP	sl 2 sts onto cn and hold in front, p2, k2 from cn

ENCHANTED COTTAGE

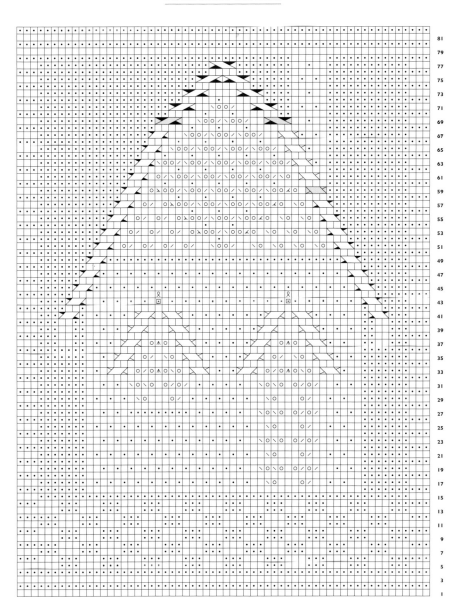

BIBLIOGRAPHY

There are a lot of books that will help you become a fearless knitter. The ones listed below are some of my favorites.

Gibson-Roberts, Priscilla A., and Deborah Robson. *Knitting in the Old Way: Designs & Techniques from Ethnic Sweaters.* Fort Collins, Colorado: Nomad Press, 2004.

Modesitt, Annie. *Confessions of a Knitting Heretic.* South Orange, New Jersey: ModeKnit Press, 2004.

Parkes, Clara. *The Knitter's Book of Yarn: The Ultimate Guide to Choosing, Using, and Enjoying Yarn.* New York: Potter Craft, 2007.

Righetti, Maggie. *Knitting in Plain English*, 2nd edition. New York: St. Martin's Griffin, 2007.

Square, Vicki. *The Knitter's Companion: Expanded and Updated.* Loveland, Colorado: Interweave, 2006.

Stanley, Montse. *Reader's Digest Knitter's Handbook.* Pleasantville, New York: The Reader's Digest Association Inc., 2001.

Vogue Knitting: The Ultimate Knitting Book. By the editors of *Vogue Knitting Magazine.* New York: Sixth & Spring, 2002.

Walker, Barbara. *A Treasury of Knitting Patterns, A Second Treasury of Knitting Patterns,* and *Charted Knitting Designs: A Third Treasury of Knitting Patterns.* Pittsville, Wisconsin: Schoolhouse Press, 1998.

————. *A Fourth Treasury of Knitting Patterns.* Pittsville, Wisconsin: Schoolhouse Press, 2001.

SOURCES FOR YARNS

Berroco Inc.
PO Box 367
14 Elmdale Rd.
Uxbridge, MA 01569
berroco.com
in Canada:
S. R. Kertzer Ltd.

Cascade Yarns
PO Box 58168
1224 Andover Pk. E.
Tukwila, WA 98188
cascadeyarns.com

Crystal Palace Yarns
160 23rd St.
Richmond, CA 94804
straw.com/cpy

Dale of Norway
4750 Shelburne Rd., Ste. 20
Shelburne, VT 05482
dale.no

Misti International Inc.
PO Box 2532
Glen Ellyn, IL 60138
mistialpaca.com

S. R. Kertzer Ltd.
50 Trowers Rd.
Woodbridge, ON
Canada L4L 7K6
kertzer.com

Tahki/Stacy Charles Inc./ Filatura di Crosa
70–30 80th St., Bldg 36
Ridgewood, NY 11385
tahkistacycharles.com

Lion Brand Yarn
135 Kero Rd.
Carlstadt, NJ 07072
lionbrand.com

INDEX